Contents

Acknowledgements

Going through life is a hazardous occupation and without help we would all be in a sorry state. I have had the good fortune to be supported by far more people than I can mention here. Firstly, without the mother I was fortunate to have I would have been nowhere so I want to dedicate these memoirs to her. She was an example to my sister and I, particularly as she was one of the people in life who did not have much support, and to bring up and educate two children on her own was an absolute marvel.

I have had five employers in my life, all of them offering different opportunities. Bob Leonard, without doubt the best farmer in Yorkshire always insisted on everything being done right and that lesson you do not forget and I still quote him today some 50 years later. On leaving college I worked for Linley Sowersby for a year when he had the good sense to sack me, the only time in my life it has happened but I learned from him the hardship of a small family farm and the sacrifices which have to be made, like not going out! We disagreed on that point. The late Maurice Tibbetts for whom I worked for three years I suppose whetted my appetite for pigs and let me do more or less what I wanted to do with them, and I have always appreciated encouragement.

The late Eric Wright with whom I worked for seven years; seven hard years in the auctioneering and farming business and he always made me think. He was forever way ahead of me and if a new rule came out or a new farm subsidy, Eric had it sussed in a very short space of time. He was the first

PIG IN A POKE
The Ramblings of a Country Peasant

Samuel King Walton

Foreword by Jeremy Skipper

Best wishes
Sam Walton

First published in 2006 by Clio Publishing,
Southampton, England.

www.cliopublishing.co.uk

A full CIP record for this book is available from the British Library.

ISBN: 0-9542650-4-1

Designed & typeset by Steve Messer, Southampton.
Printed by CPI Antony Rowe, Eastbourne.

Meaning of 'Pig in a Poke': An offering or deal that is foolishly accepted without being examined first – a phrase believed to date back to 1530.

Origin of 'Pig in a Poke': Enshrined in British commercial law as *caveat emptor*, from the Latin for 'buyer beware'; a poke is a small sack or bag and is the origin of the word pocket, just the sort of bag useful for carrying a piglet to market.

employer to have me on a profit sharing basis and that above all else sharpens the mind. He was a great help to me when I took my farm.

Harry Brown in Lincolnshire is a friend to this day in his 90th year. He always enjoyed time out and encouraged me to do the same when we were not busy which I have to say is an unusual but very effective approach. It was with Harry where I had experience of things like black currants, daffodils, sugar beet, potatoes and the early days of oil seed rape, along with milking cows through a bail.

My last employer, Mr Harold Watson-Hall, sadly died some years ago. He was a fishing magnate and a gentleman through and through, and although our aims and objects

The author, boar house, Vietnam.

were somewhat different for the farm I am ever grateful for the opportunity of managing for him for those four years, and I had my first taste of trying to meet the targets set by the management consultancy firm we employed.

All these people helped in forming my farming views, ability and achievements and I am eternally grateful to them all and hope I have done them justice along the way.

Ann and Digby Scott who own *Pig World* and with whom I have worked for 20 years, are two of my best friends. Without their enthusiasm and unstinting support, *Pig World* would never have got off the ground and would certainly not have grown and developed in the way it has. They are two of the hardest working people I know as well as two of the most intelligent and that is the finest compliment I can pay them. They have been tremendous in encouraging me to have this book published.

Jeremy Skipper who has written the foreword to this book has been a close friend ever since *Pig World* began. He used to farm pigs and for several years wrote a monthly column in *Pig Farming*. He has always kept me up-to-date with new developments in our industry and has been a leader as well. On top of that Jeremy knows how to live and that has taught me a lot also.

Now to the nitty gritty. Dr Susan England for some reason sent me a book to review about a family which kept pigs between the two World Wars. I think my reply to her in my most modest way was that I had written a few memoirs, which I thought were better! So her company Clio Publishing very kindly asked to see what I had written – from that has emerged this book. Susan now knows one or two more words than she did when we first met, and I had a devil of a job to convince her that some of my spelling mistakes were in fact

Yorkshire dialect! To Steven Messer the designer of the book for his patience when I wanted something different. My eternal thanks.

Lastly, I have to thank my immediate family for helping and supporting me along the way. Being away from home so much has not been easy and although the children are now adults, there was a time when *Pig World* first started when the father figure would be absent. That made life more difficult for Ellen with which she coped admirably. Now with two beautiful granddaughters it brings back to you the importance of family life.

My sincere thanks to all.

About the Author

Samuel King Walton was born on 2 May 1935 at South Shields, County Durham. His father, also Samuel King, was from a farming family, although not at that time farming. His mother Myra, née Ford, was the daughter of an engineer making metallic packings.

The family moved from South Shields to Hull for a while then to York where Sam's sister, Judi, was born. At the outbreak of war the family were banished to Northumberland to live in his maternal grandfather's cottage in a village called Ninebanks. At the age of six, Sam's parents divorced and he did not see his father again for a further twelve years when, by chance, at the Smithfield Show, he saw the name of a Sam Walton who had bought the champion steer and who was living in Suffolk. He took himself off to find this man who turned out to be his father. They continued to correspond and meet for a number of years, Sam senior was farming, had a demolition business and was a director of the British Livestock Export Commission which meant he went around the country buying bulls, rams and ponies for export and occasionally taking them abroad. Sam junior thinks that perhaps it was from his father that he inherited his wander-lust and his keen eye for livestock, knowing a good one from a bad one. It was the only thing he did inherit as he received not one penny piece!

Meanwhile during his junior years, Sam's mother ran the local Co-op shop in Ninebanks enabling her to support her family, something for which Sam and his sister Judi are eternally thankful. Having passed his eleven-plus at Ninebanks Primary School, Sam was all set to go to Hexham Grammar School but events overtook this plan. A family friend living in Yorkshire suggested that Myra would be ideal as housekeeper and secretary-companion to a farmer in Yorkshire and that was really the turning point in Sam's life. He went to Hull Grammar School, excelled in French and English, managed to get five O levels, did not see much point in doing A levels, so left to work on the farm where the family were living.

A year at Askham Bryan College gave him an insight to living with other people and to thinking globally instead of parochially. He was an enthusiastic member of Young Farmers, taking office as secretary after being the chairman, belonged to the local Agricultural Discussion Group which he at one time chaired, and after college took a variety of jobs on several farms. He was awarded a Young Farmers six-month exchange visit to Southern Rhodesia, which gave him an even greater insight to travel and the problems of other people. Rising through the ranks in farming saw Sam eventually take his own farm. He had always been interested in writing and broadcasting and eventually at the age of fifty, began a writing career which saw him become the founding editor of a national magazine called *Pig World*, which has enabled him to visit thirty-three different countries to study not only pigs but general agriculture, and of course culture. For a while he wrote a weekly column in a local paper that drew lots of comment from both farming and non-farming people, but unfortunately the paper folded, owing him payment for several weeks' contributions.

Married to Ellen, a farmer's daughter from Derbyshire, they have two adopted children; Romney who arrived with them on Sam's birthday in 1974, and Victor whom they collected on Ellen's birthday in 1977. Romney is married to David from Peebles but they live in Abu Dhabi where they both teach and have two beautiful daughters, Sophie Grace and Phoebe Eve, who are without doubt the apple of Sam's eye. He visits them every year, and they return the visit in the summer. He wanted to be known as Grand Pops but Sophie could not get her tongue round that so she called him Barm Pots and the name has stuck ever since.

Victor, as yet, seems to be playing the field, which as an air steward he is able to do. Sam is looking forward to the day Victor appears with one of the stunning stewardesses to be seen on all flights. As Sam says, he would like nothing better now than a beautiful daughter-in-law.

Sam does not suffer fools gladly, is appalled at the amount of red tape everyone has to deal with and feels that although he is in favour of safety for both people and food, that the boys in Whitehall and Brussels have over-cooked the goose, the goose which lays the golden egg. He is convinced that there will, in the not too distant future, be a world famine, and when the Government have completely squashed farming in the United Kingdom, in favour of imported cheaper product, we here will be amongst the first to feel the pinch, as food will no longer be cheap to import once we no longer produce at home.

Sam, 1937; always a sturdy little chap.

Foreword

I was at the same time both very surprised and honoured when I received an invitation to write the foreword to this book and found myself accepting with some humility. Of the hundreds of 'worthies' in the farming industry that Sam knows well, why me?

Sometimes the true character of a man emerges from his writings. Sometimes an entirely different individual appears from the printed text. In this case, the book shows beyond doubt that the author is himself - straightforward, down to earth, unassuming and, best of all, a proper Yorkshireman!

Most forewords are too long and mostly appreciations of what you are about to read. If I had the courage of my convictions, I would stop here and just say, 'Read it, you will thoroughly enjoy it'. However, I feel I have the right to be a little more traditional and explain a few reasons why I found this book such good reading.

Not only does it bring back some memories, many of which I had forgotten, but it also explains intelligently some of the problems associated with farming over the decades, the political interference (or indifference) and the dramatic changes we have witnessed in our lifetime. The jobs we took for granted on the farm, would simply not be allowed now under modern legislation, yet we got by, produced fantastic quality produce and survived.

Many folks, who have had a traditional upbringing in farming, have gone to college, landed a job as a farm manager and then gone on to farm on their own account. Very, very few of us in the farming industry, however, have had the courage to take the opportunities, which came Sam's way, to go off at a tangent and virtually start a completely new career in their mid-fifties.

I have only known Sam since the birth of *Pig World* and know very little of his previous existence because he never really talks about himself. To me this book is a real eye-opener as I suspect it will be to many others. What an extraordinary life he has led and I have a feeling that this book is only the tip of the iceberg.

Sam and I have enjoyed several Continental jaunts together and the first thing that struck me about Sam at work was his phenomenal memory - we would go around two or three Italian pig units and Sam would listen intently to every word spoken, ask a few questions, make virtually no notes, take a couple of photos and the next month produce 5,000 words in the magazine describing everything in perfect detail and pop in a photo of some lovely lass I missed on the way!

He is also blessed with an excellent sense of humour and I well remember one trip to Hanover by car just after I had bought a satellite navigation thingy. The 'sat-nav' took us directly without a hitch to some small hotel in the back streets of Hanover and Sam was very impressed but wanted to know what I called the young lady inside the box of tricks giving all the instructions. I said I hadn't really thought about it and all the way back home Sam kept saying that I must give her a name. The day after we got back, the phone rang and the unmistakable Yorkshire voice thundered down the line the single word: 'Freda'. I said, 'I beg your pardon, Sam, what on earth are you talking about?' 'That lass', he said, 'you've got in the car - you have to call her F-R-E-D-A...Finds Route Easily Doesn't Argue!' To this day, all sat-navs are called Freda in our family.

All professions and walks of life have their characters and the British pig industry is, indeed, very fortunate to have Sam Walton.

Jeremy Skipper, May 2006.

Preface

Tha's doing it all wrong, lad', were Sam Walton's first words as he strode into my magazine publishing office. Clearly there was no point in standing on one's dignity with this chap, so I asked him if he would mind, terribly, showing me how to do it all right. He condescended so to do.

Thus began a working relationship which has endured over twenty years, and has developed into firm friendship, and which, after much nagging from himself, led to the launch of *Pig World* magazine, which has grown to be one of the world's most respected farming publications.

When Sam told me a couple of years ago he was planning to write a book, it was my turn to say, 'Tha's got it all wrong, lad'. Nobody, I explained patiently, would be the slightest bit interested in his scribblings. But I know now't. When I read the first draft of *Pig in a Poke. The Ramblings of a Country Peasant* (which he wrote in about five minutes) I realised instantly that it was pure gold. Sam has lived through fascinating times and thanks to his unquenchable wanderlust he has seen more of life than anyone else I know.

He dissimulates when he describes himself (as he so often does) as a 'simple country peasant'. Whilst he can be a bit of a peasant at times, he is anything but simple. He has one of the most open, enquiring minds I have known; throughout his life he has been avid to see new sights and to learn new ideas. He would call himself a farmer who does a bit of scribbling. I would say he is a natural journalist, keen to pass on his experiences joyously, naturally and always honestly.

I hope you enjoy Sam's book as much as I have. If you are of a certain age, and connected with farming, you will revel in his memories, for this book positively reeks of kerosene and hard tractor seats. But don't for a minute think you have to be a farmer to enjoy *Pig in a Poke. The Ramblings of a Country Peasant.* A good read is a good read. And what Sam Walton has done here is give us all a good read. Well done, lad.

Digby Scott, July 2006

Glossary

Selected glossary of farming terms and phrases

Chaff
The small flake-like particles, which cover the grain.

Chitting
Causing the potatoes to sprout ready for planting.

Luance
A hybrid word meaning lunch and allowance.

Prill
A very small smooth coated ball-like object relating to fertiliser for even distribution instead of a granule. About 3-4 mm in diameter.

Rive/riving
To split asunder or to tear apart. Pulling at things and using excessive force.

Stook
When the sheaves of corn are placed upright together to dry.

Stubble
The amount of straw left standing after harvesting a crop.

Stubble cleaning
Cultivating the soil to kill weeds before planting the next crop.

Swathe turner
A machine for turning the swathes or rows of hay.

Theaked
A slang word for thatching.

1 | Formative Years

T hu'll heh te 'ug kaf. Those dreaded words. I can see him now, his bloodshot eyes, like piss-holes in the snow, glowering hatred, his unshaven stubble, the self-rolled fag dangling from his mean narrow lips, his face contorted in rage, his yellowing teeth clenched in a vice-like grip. This was the foreman who looked upon a fourteen year old as the lowest form of life. Carrying chaff on threshing days was, indeed, the lowest form of life and would not be allowed today, something to do with the Health and Safety Executive.

He seemed to take a delight in being a bully. I didn't realise then that like most bullies, he was also a coward, as I found out some time later. It seemed to me that Saturday mornings, half terms and holidays from school, always appeared to coincide with threshing days. There was supposed to be something romantic about threshing days. I never found it in the least bit romantic, not even in later years when having been allowed to stack the loose straw, or wire the old Reffold baler, stack bales, work on the stack itself or carry the sixteen stone sacks of corn. The hum of the machine, the fairly constant sound of the tractor exhaust, I don't go back far enough to remember threshing with a steam engine that meant very regular, repetitive actions, physical actions. I do, however, well remember being on the stack and feeding the sheaves to the man on the drum. It meant developing a rhythm of the arms as the other man on the stack threw the sheaves to me, hopefully the right way up. One particular day, I was sliding the sheaves down at the beginning of the day, from a particularly steep stack, and I guess they were arriving on the drum a shade too quickly. If the drum was fed too fast, there was a bit of a whoomph, the machine would momentarily slow down and the tractor engine would govern that little bit as it tried to drive the extra load. There was then usually a chorus from the rest of the gang, who would shout up and ask George what he was doing? The day passed fairly uneventfully, until the stack got well below the level of the machine, which meant the sheaves were then lifted a fair way up. Old George glanced over the edge from where he was cutting the sheaves open, and gently feeding each sheaf into the drum he shouted down, 'You can send them as fast as you like now!'

Next time we started a stack, I treated him with more respect, a salutary lesson.

Before anyone was allowed on a stack or to carry sacks, particularly if he was a 'lad' on a farm, they had to serve their time carrying chaff. It was a horrible job. All the dust seemed to come out in the chaff sector, sometimes the machine was drawn up between two stacks, which restricted the area available for spreading out the sheet which was usually four old sacks opened out and stitched together. Once you had managed to rake sufficient chaff onto the sheet, the four corners of the sheet had to be twisted round each other, the loaded sheet was rolled onto one side, your knee was pushed into the sheet to hold it in that position, then you ducked under your arms and half pulled the sheet onto your back, the tied corners over your shoulder, where your hands hung onto them for grim death. It was very uncomfortable carrying the sheet, for invariably it hung so low as to catch your heels whilst walking, which almost caused you to trip. If the stack was in a field the chaff could be carried a little way from the machine and burnt later. However, stacks were normally in the stack-yard, where the chaff was usually carried into the chaffhouse, which often meant going halfway up the granary steps and rolling the sheet through a hole in the wall, where the contents fell onto a heap. That was fine until the chaff grew to the height of the hole, then you had to crawl in and shove it all about. Sometimes on your way up the steps, you would meet a corn carrier on his way down and as they were much more important than a chaff carrier, you had to give way. Most farms in those days had fold yards, or cattle yards, which had a lot of tumbrils in them, from which the cattle ate. These were square wooden troughs with a leg at each corner and could be overturned by a bullock in a matter of seconds. Each threshing day, apart from filling the chaff house, the tumbrils also needed filling with the fill belly for the bullocks which was mixed with the sliced turnips grown on the farm and the inevitable molasses. To do this meant you had to go down the passageway leading to the yards, with the sheet of chaff still banging away at your heels. There was a gate to open, once through it had to be closed and then there was the yard to cross, which was usually knee-deep in straw, and did not improve the walking. As you struggled across, a bullock was sure to come behind you and push! Bullocks are very strong and a push from them meant you usually went full length. Then you had to upright the tumbrils, and provided the sheet had not come undone there was then the problem of lifting it into a tumbril, not easy for a young lad. By the time you had done all this and returned to the machine, there was more chaff there than would go in your next sheet. It was a losing battle from morning till night. At the end of a day, your shoulders were red raw, your eyes were even more bloodshot than the foreman's, your lungs were full of dust, your mouth was dry, and your nose was blocked with horrible black stuff. For many a farm worker, carrying chaff would be the start of farmer's lung and I guess I know how miners feel now, when they are all suffering from silicosis and quite rightly seeking compensation. Masks were unheard of in those days and if you put a handkerchief around your face, you were confronted with a barrage of cries from the others, calling you 'cissy'. Maybe the Health and Safety Executive have something to offer after all!

Perhaps 'luance time' was the best part of a threshing day. The word is a cross between 'lunch' and 'allowance', and was a carry-over from the war when rationing was in place. There was an allowance for such jobs, so in typically Yorkshire fashion, the hybrid word 'luance' was invented. It consisted of a cup of tea and a scone or perhaps a piece of fruit pie, which was provided either by the boss's wife, or the foreman's wife. This appeared regularly at nine in the morning and at three in the afternoon. Threshing always started at seven in the morning, so it was more than a welcome break. However, if your chaff was not all cleared away when the machine stopped for a break, it was an opportunity to catch up. Many a time I have just got it cleared before they started up again, and if I went to have a drink to slake my parched throat, often there was no tea left, someone else had eaten the scone and the foreman would smirk. I think he was sadistic too. It was not a pleasant moment, in fact it was soul destroying, but as my dear old mother used to say, never mind son, it is character building.

Wheat chaff was the most plenteous and stored in the chaff house as was oat chaff, although there was less of that to carry. I could never decide whether the barley awns which got into every nook and cranny of your body, and some you didn't know you had, were worse to carry than either pea or bean chaff. None of them were particularly good. There wasn't an excessive amount from any of them, but the peas and beans were just like irritating dust. Barley chaff was usually carried away into the orchard or an adjacent field for burning, so at least we didn't have the toil of the chaff house or the bullock yards. Sometimes the bullocks had pea and bean chaff, but it was mostly burnt.

I remember one day when I was struggling a bit with some particularly plentiful wheat chaff, and taking it into the bullock yard it was soon building up , the machine was between two stacks and no doubt I was losing! The foreman came along and said, 'I don't know what you are playing at, but Dennis can carry the chaff and the pulls as well'. The pulls were the short straws that came out at the end of the machine, under the straw walkers. At one time there was also someone carrying them away, which was one stage better than carrying the chaff, and eventually when balers came in, in place of the old loose straw elevator, the pulls were then elevated into the baler. However, on this day I had really had enough. The last thing I wanted was hassle from the foreman who checked each department of the threshing gang, throwing his weight around, being sarcastic and belittling.

When he mentioned to me that Dennis could do both jobs, I threw the sheet down, and suggested to him that perhaps he should fetch Dennis? No one had ever spoken to him like that, his jaw dropped open and he just turned and walked away.

There were three other incidents I can well remember which put him in his place good and proper. We grew a lot of potatoes in those days, sort of second earlies, which were picked by a gang of women from Hull. Most of them came from the fishing fraternity and were a close-knit community. Lots of them were related and no doubt most of the money they earned would be spent in their local at night. They usually had their hair in curlers and wore headscarves, and perhaps even tried to smoke a cigarette as they worked. The conversation would revolve around drinking, partying, and which particular fellow they had had their eye on the previous evening and what they weren't half going to do to him that evening! They had a stretch each, between two sticks, and as the Wallace digger did its rounds, one row at a time, up one side and back down the other, the women would move on each time to the next stretch. I always thought they worked like hell and did a grand job. The foreman used to come into the field and bully them, cajole them, try to drive them on. There was never a word of encouragement. One day he came along, scowled at the leader, a Mrs Busby, whom everybody called 'auntie' and made the mistake of saying to her, 'Potato pickers, I have shit them'. Auntie straightened up, looked straight into his bloodshot eyes and replied, 'If your arse is as big as your mouth, I will believe you'. Again his jaw dropped open, and he turned on his heels and left. The gang had no further problem with him. It was at this moment I realised he was also a coward. Another day we were trying to loaden some bullocks. Instead of allowing the bullocks to take their time and feel their way out of the yard, he laid into them mercilessly with a stick, beating the hell out of them. One of the men grabbed the stick from him, caught him by the throat and threatened to do the same to him if he so much as used a stick again. He went pale and backed down. I also remember an occasion when I was leading sheaves and forking to an elderly man on the wagon, and drawing the tractor on between stooks myself, when for some reason the tractor engine died. Try as I might, I could not get the damned thing going again, and in those days it was a handle start and paraffin engines. Eventually, the foreman rolled up, wondering where the load was. He flew into a rage, grabbed me by the throat and threw me to the ground, swearing and calling me all the names under the sun. I was fifteen years old. Old Tom on the load, slid down at a speed that would have shamed a younger man, grabbed the foreman by the shoulder and swung him round. He looked him straight in the eye and said, 'If I catch you bullying that lad once more, I will swing for you. And if you are spoiling for a fight, find someone your own size'. I had no more physical aggravation from the foreman, but at every opportunity he would give me all the rotten jobs to do.

Today, of course, such tactics would not be allowed or encouraged. The idea of driving staff has long gone. Men in those days were probably living in a tied cottage, without any facilities, were afraid of losing their jobs, and I fear were taken advantage of whereas today, men are much more a part of a farming business, where encouragement and leadership is more important. Many farms have financial incentives, is there any better way?

Thinking back to how we grew potatoes, I have mentioned the Wallace digger. This was a simple elevator, with a share that was set to go under the rows. The soil supposedly dropped through the elevator web and the potatoes went over the back, along with the potato tops. If we were lifting green tops, the discs at the front of the digger often used to become clogged and stop going round, which meant that the soil simply heaped up in front of the digger, causing the Fergy to develop wheel spin, that only aggravated the situation. One of the jobs I had was to sit on a piece of wood, which was placed across the elevator section, my feet on the shanks, that supported the discs, and I had to try to release any impending obstruction. I never thought of it as being dangerous, you simply got on and did it. I imagine these days the farmer would probably be fined or imprisoned for allowing such practices.

When I look at a modern combine at work my mind often goes back to the laborious way we used to do the harvesting. I can still remember working with horses, although just after the war, the old Fordson, Case, and Allis Chalmers tractors were beginning to take over. They all had what now would look like narrow tyres and quite easily sink in a wet hole. I was always intrigued by binders: sheaf after sheaf neatly tied (well mostly). Corners of fields were mown out by hand so that neither the horses nor tractors would make a mess when turning the first time round. It was a slow old job. Stooking also took a long time. Funnily enough, I quite liked stooking. We always built the stooks facing North and South, so that the sun shone on both sides during the day. There was a lot of pride in making neat stooks and having them in straight rows. The short part of the end of the sheaf was always on the inside, which meant the knot on the string, that tied the sheaves, was on the outside. Wheat would usually be stoked six sheaves per side, barley in fives.

Depending on the weather, by the time we had all the crops cut and stooked, we could begin leading. Often we had a horse pulling the trailers on in the field from stook to stook, whilst a tractor would take the loads up to the yard. Finding gears on the tractors sometimes took longer than forking the stook on to the trailer. So there could be up to four men to one trailer, two forking and two loading. There was immense pride taken in building a straight load and I always remember that the last load at night would be what was called a 'moonlighter' and would be particularly high. I always enjoyed loading sheaves - it was a real skill. Occasionally, a load slipped slightly and would have to be taken home very steadily. If ever anyone did build a load which fell over, then he was in for a ribbing from his mates for some considerable time. I once remember when I was leading home, by that time it was with a Fergy, a load, which to put it kindly didn't really stand much chance of getting there and had a fair list to port. It was roped down well to the trailer and I went very steadily. On the way up to the yard, I avoided where possible the potholes or slack places on the track, but to no avail. About a hundred yards from home, not only did the load slip, but it took the trailer with it. Of course it twisted the drawbar and the Fergy had one wheel off the ground. I had a sinking feeling in my stomach as I approached the foreman to tell him of the good news that he had made the load!

One thing I do remember from those days was that all stubbles were very clean. We did not seem to have the weeds we do today and wild oats were practically unheard of. Men would spend the summer months 'looking' the corn, which meant they carried a hoe, walked all the crops whilst striking out any weeds, such as docks and thistles. The corn was cut much sooner with a binder than it was with a combine, so any weeds which did survive would be cut before they matured. Now, as you watch the combine, it throws everything on to the ground, the chaff, the pulls, the straw, and any rubbish we have grown. Stubble cleaning did not exist in those days. Stubbles were simply ploughed as soon as possible and very often they were ploughed up as far as the stooks had been removed. It was, I believe, quite common talk in the local on a Saturday night, to see which farm had got the most ploughing done, and who had got nearest to the stooks.

Stacking was a very skilled job. On reflection all the jobs done by hand required an inordinate amount of skill and sometimes strength, and threshing days in particular called for a lot of stamina. Men were well-muscled, very strong and fit and seldom ailed anything and yes, we all ate a lot of very fat bacon! There is nothing like hard work for burning off fat. There was no need to do idiotic jogging or go to a gym and pump iron or whatever the latest fitness fad is, doubt if those things were even thought of then. Having said that, it is now patently obvious that some of the physical tasks have taken their toll on many men. Rheumatism from working in wet conditions and back problems from constantly carrying up to as much as nine-teen stones in sacks, are two common things found, along with the previously mentioned farmer's lung. One prime example of this (in fact two really) when I cast my mind back, is the, foreman. I had not seen him since I was eighteen, until I came across him one day sitting on a seat in Beverley Market Square. Some twenty-five years had elapsed, so he would have been in his late sixties. I hardly recognised him, he was gaunt, his eyes were sunken and his breathing was bad, very chesty indeed. He said how pleased he was to hear that I had managed to start on my own some years prior to this meeting, and how he knew I always would. He said that he realised now that he had made a big mistake in always riving on and rushing about and not taking care of himself or others, and how we was suffering from it now. He said he was 'buggered'. I thought he looked awful and was staring death in the face. He died a month later, a bitter, broken man.

The other example concerned an employee on the last farm I managed before I took my present farm as a tenant. Let us assume that this particular chap was called John. He was quite a character, remained a bachelor all his life, grew roses and on-ions as a hobby, had plenty of money, but always came to work looking like a tramp. He had a very old cycle that squeaked as he rode along, the pedals had long since lost their rubber and several spokes were missing. When John eventually disposed of his chariot as he called it, it went to York Museum! When I first arrived on the farm the owner told me I could do what I liked, and could sack anyone except John. When I asked what was so special about John, he told me, while laughing, that he was the only chap we have who can knock two gate posts down at once! What he really meant by this I think was that John had worked on the farm since leaving school and could do most jobs. Indeed at that time, we had a Vicon fertiliser spreader, the instruction book for which had long been lost. No one but John had any idea how to set the damned thing, but if I sent him to top dress a field, he would come out of the gate as the last prill fell out of the spout. All he had was a nail and a piece of string!

After I had been there two weeks, I arrived one morning on the farm which housed the pigs and the dairy cows, plus one of the corn stores. It had quite a large flat area of concrete, which appeared to me to be three inches deep in water after a heavy rain storm. None of the other men had any idea where the drains were for this section, but they all said, 'John will know'. Sure enough, up comes John, his usual five minutes late, cycle squeaking and grinding away. I looked at him for inspiration and he said. 'Come out of the way, I know what is up with this'. He laid his cycle down, walked to an area of the concrete, put his hands under the water and fiddled about until he found the cast iron man-hole top. He somehow managed to prise this up then slid himself into the man-hole until he was up to his waist in water. He plunged his hand further down and retrieved a tennis ball that was blocking one of the outlet pipes. There was a gurgle and the water began to disappear from the concrete. He was of course soaked to the skin, and covered in sewage too, as it was part of that particular system from one of the houses. So there was John, looking very bedraggled but very pleased with himself. I simply said, 'Thank you John, I had better take you home and you can have a bath and get dried out and cleaned up'. 'No', he replied, 'I shall be alright'. When I saw John in Beverley quite recently he was crippled up with rheumatism and walking slowly with two sticks. He is now in a home and being looked after, spending most of his time confined to a wheel chair. But more about John in a later chapter.

Believe me, there are no such thing these days as heroics in farming.

Harvesting is a subject that has been painted many times by artists. Before the days of elevators, a contraption called a monkey was used to pass the sheaves , before they in turn were passed to the men on the stack. A monkey consisted of a platform on two legs, which was reared up against a stack, the load pulling up alongside. Elevators were a great stride forward as they eliminated the use of another man. Before my time, stacks would be thatched, or as they say in East Yorkshire, 'theaked'. It was nice to see and now and then the odd 'theaked' stack would still appear on some of the more traditional farms. Towards the end of the stacking regime, it was more common just to cover the stacks well with loose straw and put a net over them. I think perhaps there was more pride taken in stacking than any other job on the farm. I have seen some of the old hands, in their own time, walk around a stack they had built and clip the long ends of the bottom of the sheaves, just to make the stack look tidy.

Stacks of course were a panacea for vermin. It was very advisable to tie your trouser bottoms with string. I can't imagine anything much worse than having a rat run up your trouser leg - on the inside! Rat catching was great sport. As they seem to breed continually, it was common to uncover a nest with rats from as young as day olds, up to grandparents. Farm dogs had a field day and I remember towards the end of the threshing regime we used to run a wire net around the stack in order to catch as many of the filthy things as we could. If a rat can escape, it will do. If you corner it, it is not a pretty sight with its teeth bared, and letting out the sort of scream only a rat can. It sent shivers up and down your spine. I have twice had a nasty experience along those lines, once when I found a rat had fallen into a corn bin with a tapered bottom. I bravely went down the ladder to the bottom of the bin where the rat was leaping at me fiercely and screaming blue murder. Another occasion occurred one evening when I was checking my pigs with my two Jack Russells, Sooty and Sweep, in attendance. They were superb ratters and liked nothing better. I entered one of the farrowing houses to find a large rat running along a ledge near the inside eaves. I struck at it with my stick, sort of caught it and it jumped down on to my face, before hitting the deck and meeting its doom. It still makes me shiver when I think of it. Rats are definitely not my most favourite animal.

I have never quite worked out why we have rats. I suppose they are all part of nature's food chain, like wood pigeons, which seem to serve no useful purpose, other than grazing my oil seed rape. I well remember one evening on the farm where John worked we decided we would have a ratting session. Charlie the pig man was convinced we had a lot of rats under the granary floor in a false ceiling, and above one of his finisher pens. We were not supposed to have rats as we paid Rentokil to keep the farms baited. A couple of the chaps witth Charlie, myself, and my then dog Rip, fastened ourselves in the piggery, blocked up all means of escape, plugged the holes up in the granary, which were alongside the wall, and began to take down the false ceiling. There must have been two inches of corn husks and rat droppings. It soon became obvious that we did indeed have a colony of rats, a very thriving colony of rats. Some fell down as we gently took out the false ceiling where Rip had a field day. By the end of the evening we had a full barrow of dead rats, 157 in total, of which the dog had killed 53. He was about exhausted. Next day I rang Rentokil, asked for the manager and told him I had a problem, which I felt would best be discussed with him, rather than one of his henchmen. I have always believed that you should speak to the butcher and not the chopping block. He duly arrived and was invited to look at the dead rats. As a result, I believe we were given a considerable rebate on the contract, or perhaps even free rodent control for a while. I know he came down himself several times after that, to make certain that we were receiving 'effective' rodent control.

I suppose apart from Jack Russells, which are along with collie dogs, my favourite animals, the next favourite would be pigs. Pigs are without doubt highly intelligent, very akin to humans from an anatomical point of view, and respond better than most humans. Pigs have always played a major role in my working life. Little did I think that one day I would be involved in the setting up of a national pig magazine, become its editor and have years of wonderful travel, fun and friendship that it has afforded me.

I come from a farming family who are all sheep and cattle men in Northumberland and Cumberland. However, my parents divorced when I was six years old so I had to start from the bottom, and you can't get much lower than carrying chaff! Nonetheless, I never doubted that one day I would farm on my own account and in 1973, just before my birthday, I was awarded the tenancy of Village Farm in Driftield where I now live. It was only seven miles from the farms I was managing on the outskirts of Beverley at the time, so it was quite handy for me during the hand-over period to my successor, who incidentally managed said farms until he retired some twenty-eight years later. When I left college, I decided it would probably take a number of years to achieve the tenancy of my own farm, so thought I might as well experience as many branches of farming as possible. I had looked at two farms to let prior to Village Farm coming on the market. In both cases I just knew I would not be accepted, but as soon as I set foot on this farm, I knew it would come to me. I am not the slightest bit superstitious, but I picked up a horseshoe as I walked into the first field. I don't think I have ever seen so many people walking around a farm. Eventually there were 107 applicants. Obviously, some of the locals had seen me and kept asking if I had heard anything. I truthfully replied that I had not, so they then came to the conclusion that I must be on the short list as they had been informed they were not likely to be considered.

I well remember whilst doing something on one of the farms I was managing having a premonition that I should return to the farmhouse. As I went into the kitchen, the phone rang and it was the agent asking if he could come and see me in half-an-hour! The landlord of Village Farm wanted to get the job finalised that day, and if I had not been available I might have been out of luck. Later that day we shook hands.

The first thing I did was go and see my boss, who lived a few miles away. He had a very successful fishing business, whilst at the same time building up his four farms, which totalled approaching 1,000 acres. We sat for quite some time over a glass of whiskey. He wished me well but asked if I would consider staying on until we had appointed a successor. I had to give three months notice in any case. It took all of this time to find a successor, who also had to give three months notice. Thus, from the January, when I first knew about Village Farm it took until August to have the new man installed. That suited me fine as it meant I had a salary until my first harvest was available.

*　　*　　*

Just after the end of the war, my Mother, sister and I moved from the tiny cottage we had lived in, at a place called Ninebanks in Northumberland, to my adopted county of York-shire. Mother had been taken on as housekeeper and secretary companion to an excellent farmer on a superb farm. It was on this farm where my experiences of threshing and farming jobs had taken place and I didn't regret one minute of it. The farmer and his two sons could not have been better mentors. There was nothing they could not do and were always pleased to show you how to master any job.

Before we left Northumberland, I had just passed my elev-en-plus exam, or whatever it was called in those days, to go to Hexham Grammar School. As we were moving it meant a new

Sam and Judi outside Clinthill with a 'borrowed' dog.

Clinthill, Ninebanks where Sam,and his mother and sister, lived (cottage on the left) for most of the war years.

school, so I was duly enrolled at Hull Grammar School. I left home every school morning at ten minutes past seven, cycled just over a mile to the village to catch the seven-thirty bus to Hull, then I either walked a mile from there, or caught a trolleybus followed by a half-mile walk. In those days, nothing was thought of such a journey to school, safety was never even an issue. Today, parents are fearful of letting their children out of their sight for a second and as far as walking or cycling to school, it is a non-starter, everyone has to go by car, which only adds to the global warming we are constantly being warned about.

When my sister and I lived in Northumberland, we would walk to school every day, almost a mile, and some of the pupils walked three miles or more from the most remote farms you can imagine. I suppose children then were a bit hardier than the modern generation. Clinthill, the name of the cottage where we lived, was actually my maternal grandfather's country retreat to which we had been banished at the outbreak of

war, from South Shields, where I was born and where grandfather had his engineering business, which is still in operation
under the guidance of a cousin.

The toilet was an earth affair at the bottom of the garden.
We had two sources of water; one from a spring which was
for drinking and had to be carried a bucketful at a time from
a distance of a hundred yards, and soft water from a syke, or
underground stream which actually ran under the cottage, but
was only accessible from a distance and had to be carried. I can
still taste the spring water now, as pure as the driven snow.
The latter was also a feature of the weather in those days. It
was nothing to have drifts twelve feet deep and to be cut off
for days on end. I remember some soldiers during the war, cutting the drifts away by hand, and when they started some of
them hung their coats on the telephone wires that ran past the
house, to emphasise the depth of the drifts.

We used to love the snow. Sledging was great fun. It would
take what seemed an eternity for little legs to drag the sledge

Sam and Judi with their sledge at Clinthill, c. 1943.

to the top of a hill that was soon forgotten as we zoomed down again at great speeds. All the fields had stone walls around them, which meant the snow would pile up against them and freeze hard enough to carry a sledge as it hurtled downwards, so that we literally took off over the walls, like a modern ski jump. It could be minus quite a few degrees but you know we never ever felt the cold. There was no television in those days, only an old steam radio operated by accumulators. A firm called J. Stanley Penny called in an old Morris van every Tuesday, to collect the run down accumulators and bring us back the newly charged ones. Of course there was no electricity, and water was heated by a fire in an old black-leaded stove affair with a copper at the side. Bath night was Friday in the inevitable tin bath. The old paraffin lamps we used on a regular basis are now fetching a fortune when converted to electricity. Still they served a purpose and we knew nothing better. We had to make our own amusements. If today's younger generation had to do that I'm not sure where they would begin without

Sam – ready for the fray!

Togetherness.

a can of coke, a packet of crisps, a Big Mac, or whatever other junk food is around plus the inevitable mobile phone or MP3 player! A bus passed on a Tuesday to go to Hexham as it was market day, but returned from there at three-thirty in the afternoon and came again on a Saturday when there was actually a late bus back. If we were good, but only if we were very good, we would be allowed to go on the bus on a Saturday, maybe twice a year we visited the cinema.

My sister and I spent hours down by the river West Allen, which ran at the bottom of a steep hill behind us, about half-a-mile away. We poked sticks under rocks, watched fascinated by the trout which frequented the river and we actually caught some now and then, if we were clever enough and they were above a certain size. These days, parents would be afraid their offspring might drown. We also walked miles over the fells. We learnt to miss the bogs of which there were numerous; it was usually sensible to follow sheep tracks. Although I believe sheep are the most senseless creatures on earth, in that part of the world perhaps they recognise the difference between perishing to death or survival. A couple of miles above the cottage, way up on the fell tops, there is a large circular outcrop of huge stones, known locally as the Carrs. It stretches quite a way and I believe it was formed by an eruption of some kind many thousands of years ago. I try to go back to Ninebanks every second year or so, and I always gaze in awe at this spectacle. If anyone feels inclined to see this wonderful view it can be found on the road between Allendale and Carrshields,

We thought nothing of walking all day, then it came naturally, I suppose it was Hobson's choice. I spent hours with Les, who farmed next door, he taught me how to lamb an ewe, milk a cow, shear sheep and dip them, so many things. I must have drunk gallons of uncooled milk, straight from the cow. I remember being shown how to tuck my head into the cow's flank to prevent her kicking. Squeezing and drawing on the teats was hard work for little arms. An array of cats used to sit in the old tie up cowshed, patiently waiting for their milk,

Les Coulson with wife Doris and son Derek, 2006.

Sam beside the moat at Bewick Hall with Bess, c.1949.

which was usually administered by a stream of milk from a teat, direct into their mouths! I used to love doing that.

Les and his father had two shire horses, which I can see now, Prince and Smiler. I was allowed to drive them even at my tender age. It was great fun making hay, long before balers were even thought of. It was a laborious task but people seemed to enjoy it. I realise now how much more patient farmers were then, as things could only move slowly with horses. I was never allowed to sit on a reaper, far too young, but I could work the hayrake and the swathe turner and the sweep. One thing I did like was the introduction of what were termed 'motor bogeys'. These were old Austin or Riley motor cars with only the bonnet, windscreen and chassis, on which were built detachable bodies for fetching the pikes home, and later for carting the manure out. So here I was at the age of eight, having my first driving experience, it was great.

Les is now in his eighties, his son Derek does the farming and Les is, as he says, 'on for the Queen now', meaning he draws his pension. I reckoned up once that during his working life when the farm, the outlying fields, and part of the fell were walked every day and sometimes twice, he has traversed over 250,000 miles. Needless to say, that along with an impish sense of humour, he is still extremely fit and has never seen a doctor.

But nothing is forever. It is quite sad to see what I call rural decay in this lovely area. Once every farm had milking cows, and there would be a local chap who had an old Bedford lorry that was used on a daily basis for collecting the milk from each holding, in churns which had been filled with milk that had been run over an old cooler, serviced by water from a stream or spring or well. There were no mains water supply then, but of course there is today, as the old water system is deemed 'unsafe'. What a load of rubbish!

A farm of 60 acres is no longer a viable unit, no one milks anymore in the area, it is just down to beef and sheep. Farms have amalgamated, steadings have been sold off to city types as holiday homes, the old buildings are no longer required and some are falling down. The stone walls or dykes as they are called are also falling down whereas years ago they would have been properly maintained. Instead we see a piece of wood or a hurdle stuck into the gap. Thistles seem to have taken over, life is not the same and modern pressures have caught up. The village school, where I spent six happy years is now a house; the children, if there are any, now go by bus to another town. There is no local vicar, no shop left, which my mother ran for a number of years. Anyone interested in history might like to visit the village of Ninebanks, it has an ancient Peel Tower, well worth a visit.

My paternal grandfather used to farm Ouston, the biggest farm in the area, some 3,500 acres, where he bred Highland cattle and Galloways, to which were mated a white Shorthorn

Peel Tower, Ninebanks, 2006.

bull to produce the famous blue-grey suckler cows. There was
of course no succession of tenancy in those days so the farm
reverted to the landlord. From what I can gather, farming in
grandfather's day was not exactly a bed of roses either. When
he took the farm in 1921 he had stock worth £30,000. Due to
the slump and contagious abortion, this sum was reduced in
twelve months to nearer £3,000 - it nearly broke him. The farm
also carried a lot of sheep. I never met my grandfather, more is
the pity. An advertisement for British Telecom asks with whom
you would like to have a one-to-one conversation? For me it
would be grandfather Walton. He was by all accounts a superb
judge of livestock. A calm, quiet man, well thought of in the
area and when invited to judge at Smithfield, he declined in favour of another man whom he suggested should do it, not that
he felt unable or unwilling, but that the other man was more
worthy and deserved the opportunity. He was also I believe a
very tactful man. It was quite common then for all the farmers
to help each other with such things as clipping and dipping.

Grandfather had a large dipping set up near the road that led to the house. He had at that time a new young shepherd, who had an equally new young sheep dog. As the sheep was being herded, this young chap kept shouting and waving his arms about, no doubt trying to impress. His dog, as a result, was also excited and kept barking. He was asked several times to keep quiet, control his dog, and let the sheep find their way naturally, even if slowly. However, this was too much for the new man, he couldn't help himself, he kept on shouting and waving. At that moment the postman passed by on his cycle, so grandfather shouted to him to leave the mail and he would take it home at lunchtime. The postman also brought the local paper, which was the *Hexham Courant*. The new man continued to shout, despite Grandfather's patient pleading, so eventually he said to the lad, 'Just take this paper and that dog of thine into the shepherd's hut there, and look through the situations vacant!'

Sam and Judi with their mother opposite Clinthill, c. 1943.

Things have not only changed in hill farming, but perhaps even more so in the lowlands. Life generally now is not what it used to be, and many times people say to me that there is no longer any fun or enjoyment in farming. It seems as if we are now walking a tight rope. We have targets to meet, not only physical output, but financial as well. Everything revolves around money. We have a lot less people involved in farming, much more machinery and automation, which require a different sort of skill, but it costs money, a lot of it. We never worked during the night years ago as both horses and men had had enough by five in the afternoon. Now combining, and yes, even cultivations, are often carried out well into the next day. Why? Because we are managing with less and less labour, using bigger and bigger machinery, therefore believing that we have to justify it.

Grandfather's farm today.

2 | Technical Advances

ow wrong can you be? When the little grey Ferguson appeared, with the same engine as the Standard Vanguard car, along with its unique hydraulic system, tipping trailers, muck fillers, weeders, ploughs, cultivators, transport boxes, so many things, I really thought we had gone as far as we could go, and how modern we were.

It was the introduction of mounted implements rather than trailed ones that probably were one of the greatest advances ever made in agriculture. There are still many around now almost sixty years later. I can't see our modern fleet lasting that length of time. These tractors, although they had a starting handle for emergencies, also had electric starters. They were nippy, easy to drive, and with their independent wheel brakes were quite manoeuvrable. I wish I had a pound note for every hour I have sat on a tractor without a cab in all weathers, and particularly on the older tractors, which had cast iron seats, you would often go home with the word 'Ford' imprinted on your backside! Cabs were a later development. Before they appeared, it was common practice to grab an empty corn sack, either to sit on or put across your knees and sometimes across the shoulders. We thought nothing of it at the time, but like a lot more things that sort of behaviour has also taken its toll on a lot of former farm workers.

Combines and sprayers soon began to appear. My first experience of a combine was a Massey 21, which had a very thirsty Chrysler petrol engine. There was no power steering, all the corn was bagged on a platform and kneed across from there to trailers where it was taken home to the farm and carried up the granary, or if it needed drying there were one or two tray driers in the area. The operator had a hard job on this combine. If he needed to lift the reel, then he put his foot on a pedal, which released the hold, and then he had to turn a rather clumsy wheel by hand which in turn raised the reel. Later of course electric lifting came into play, but if it was used a lot the battery would go flat. With the advent of hydraulic lifts, life became a lot easier. When tanker combines appeared, well, it was like living in a new world. Soon it was possible to do two tonnes per hour, and balers began to appear. The whole aspect of farming changed. Little was I to know just how far we would go, and particularly with electronics and now of course computers and satellites. However, I sometimes think the 1950s were a more preferred era. Certainly there was not the pressure on us like there is at present. We did not have the rules and regulations we now have, but I like to think that at that time common sense was creeping in, and that we didn't do too many daft things. It was an exciting time, an enjoyable time, the actual physical act of farming was very satisfying.

It appears to me that as farming practices have become more sophisticated so the amount of legislation has increased. The annoying aspect about this development is that they are generally designed by people who have no concept of farming, are completely lacking in 'nous', and are probably empire-building. I remember once on a farm where I was working we had an Allis Chalmers baler that made small, neat bales like sausages. For it to comply with the safety code, or for it to be guarded as it was supposed, meant rendering the machine totally unusable. This is precisely the sort of thing that I find frustrating. I am all for safety and well-being at work, and for safe and traceable food, but let's not go too far. In many ways we are completely over the top, and if we continue as we are it will be dangerous to get out of bed in a morning. We will probably all finish up living in a glass cage!

* * *

I suppose I was an average pupil at school. I thoroughly
enjoyed learning French, was reasonable at English language,
and Geography. I didn't get on well with the Maths teacher,
who also took us for Music. Now I like music but I can't read a
note of it, I never have any idea of what it is, or who the com-
poser might be. I don't think that matters, but ask me to take
a music test and I am sunk. I once got 2% in a music examina-
tion for drawing a minim! However, I managed to get five O
levels, did not want to stay on at sixth form, so left at sixteen to
work for a year full time on the farm where we lived. I couldn't
wait. There was always something new to do; the family were
undoubtedly leaders in agriculture and still are to this day.
Their farms are totally immaculate in every respect. At this
time, pigs and poultry, potatoes and peas were all the rage in
Holderness. I gained experience with free-range poultry and
deep litter. I well remember finding some deep litter hens with
their rear ends all eaten away. It was not a pretty sight. At first
we thought it was rats, but could find no evidence of entry.
Eventually we spotted a couple of hens that had turned can-
nibal, a problem that was to beset many a unit. We finished up
de-beaking the hens, which helped considerably, but did not
cure the underlying problem. Later on, plastic 'spectacles' with
solid lenses were fitted to them, which also helped. As time
progressed the industry learnt about the nutrition of hens and
what needed to be in the litter, and we used to throw turnips,
or kale stalks in to them, anything to keep them occupied. I
can't think that hen cannibalism is a problem these days.

Pigs were housed in a variety of buildings and straw yards.
Sows were farrowed outside in wooden huts. It was great fun
trying to round up the pigs, which inevitably escaped at wean-

ing. We knew nothing then of litters per sow per year, farrowing rate, numbers of sows per boar, there were no recording schemes to go by, just a pencil and notebook for the very sophisticated units. I learnt how to castrate pigs, a job I think I excelled at, and although I have not done any now for at least fifteen years, I have never forgotten how, and could do it again at the drop of a hat. Things like pig advisers began to appear, but they were all actually salesmen from feed companies. Trials were done on different rations and I shudder to think what growth rates and gradings were. Bullocks were also a part of the mixed farming, along with sheep. One thing I did not like doing was castrating lambs before the rubber rings arrived. That was when we used an old razor blade, let into a cork from a bottle. The lambs were held up in front of you, their legs folded so as one front and one back were held in each hand. Having made an incision, the testicles were actually drawn out by your teeth! I never seemed to develop the appetite for that. In turn, I worked on all the sectors before being accepted at Askham Bryan College at York, the following year.

I well remember feeling very apprehensive as I entered Askham Bryan College for the first time and began to meet my fellow students. Many of them were farmer's sons, some of whom would never have carried chaff, and probably lived on a different planet from myself. However, it didn't turn out to be a problem, we all gelled fairly well, but I must say that those who got into trouble the most, or did the most outlandish things, were the well-to-do sons. Our principal, Mr Jack Lindsay was a dour Scot and a disciplinarian *extraordinaire*. Looking back he was quite right. That had never been a problem to me, but it was to many of them. It was interesting to see how they reacted. If any of us stepped out of line, the punishment was double digging at six in the morning on some very hard ground. It was no use thinking that you could get away with it, because 'Happy Jack' as he was nicknamed would be there to see you start. It didn't do any of us any harm.

College courses then were very basic and unless you went to Cirencester, or Harper Adams, or similar, the only qualification available was a National Certificate in Agriculture. I had only once wavered from my desire to farm when for a while I harboured ideas of becoming a veterinary surgeon. Quite simply I could not afford to go to College for five years, so I abandoned the idea. Of course had I succeeded, I would no doubt have made a lot more money.

Lectures at college were from nine in the morning until one in the afternoon. All students had to work on a rota in all the different sections, one week on mornings, the next week on afternoons. The college had a pedigree Ayrshire herd, a pedi-

At Askham Bryan College with friend, Sir John Christopher Smith Dodsworth, known as 'Dodders'.

gree Aberdeen Angus herd, a pedigree Large White herd, plus a poultry unit, a sheep flock and a large horticultural section. Crops were cereals, sugar beet, and potatoes. So we had a fair grounding on the basics of most things, plus we had tuition on tractor driving, machinery maintenance, nutrition (such as was known then), and grassland management. I was in one of the groups that planted a copse on the farm and today as I drive past, I look at that and remind myself that it was planted in November 1952!

We were not allowed out during the week and had to be in by ten at night on Saturdays. Bicycles were encouraged, cars were not allowed, not that many of us had them then, but a couple of lads who did had them stored in the village and would in fact nip out at nights. I too nipped out on many an occasion, there were one or two of the opposite sex in the local village whom we had met at church, so it meant shin-ning up the drainpipe on my return. I remember one night, a pal of mine knew I was going out and as a prank, locked my bedroom window from the inside after I had gone. Naturally I couldn't get in and was just wondering what to do, when I noticed a window open in the bathroom on my floor level. I shinned up the pipe and as I drew level with the window, an-other friend was standing having a pee. You should have seen his face when mine appeared in front of him as I said, 'Now you bugger!'

At the end of each term a dance was held to which either the local hospital nurses or students from a teacher training college would be invited. Looking back it was hilarious as members of staff would position themselves at the doors, so that no one could actually leave the dance! How different things are now, I shudder to think what happens, or am I just a little envious? I remember once several of us did manage to 'escape', and we took some of the young women to see the bull. One of the lads nipped to the horticultural section, pinched some strawberries and we skimmed the cream off the top of the milk tank. That was a night to remember and I don't think they ever found out why the milk from the beloved Ayrshires had produced, for one day, rather watery milk.

Several years after we left, a letter was circulated asking alumni what they had learnt at Askham Bryham? I can distinctly remember replying that it had taught me to think and to live with other people and that was all. I felt that the points of an Aberdeen Angus were totally irrelevant, but anything that makes you think has to be good. I believe it made us look beyond our own back yard, that each of us, and from whatever farm, was part of a national scene. Since then, apart from being part of Europe, we are also very much part of a global scenario, or at least that is the excuse merchants use when buying our produce which according to them is for 'nowt' from overseas.

I recall several years ago, going back for a reunion at the College for our year. Some of the lads were still recognisable, some looked much older than their years, and time had dealt gently with others. We were given an address by the then principal, Mr. Pollard, about what courses they were running and how the college had grown and what kind of students they had. When it came to question time, I asked him what he did about discipline? His answer was, 'Absolutely nothing'. His view was that if students want to learn then the opportunity is there. If they can afford to come and waste time, then it was their loss. I was not convinced that he was altogether right and I told him so. I think we all need discipline of some sort, as I am sure it stands you in good stead in later life. As I write this I am aware that I have a great deal of discipline in my life, as every twentieth of the month I have to have all the copy and advertising for *Pig World* ready and available. Now that is a discipline.

I think that when we left college, we all felt we could rush out and manage any farm anywhere. Several of the students did take management jobs and succeeded very well. I felt I needed experience on a smaller farm instead of the big arable unit I had been on. I took a job not too far from York, on a small farm, approximately 80 acres with dairy cows and some finisher pigs. I was there for only a year. It was the most miserable year of my life and I think the only time when I was truly unhappy. I hated it and no matter how I tried I just could not get into it in any way. The people who owned it had been married for twenty-three years and had never had a day off. It was that kind of place and they didn't think I should either, or even go out for that matter.

I have always been interested in travel. Travel as they say broadens the mind. I was invited to join Roos Young Farmers [1] when I was fifiteen, which I did. I remember going to the first meeting. Ken Grant was the chairman and he asked a member to propose a vote of thanks, then without warning asked me to second it. I thought the end of the world had come, but thank you Ken, it actually gave me confidence, which hopefully I have retained and built on. We were given training on livestock judging and public speaking. One year I won the fat lamb judging and was selected to go to Smithfield. Another year we won the public speaking cup and when I was twenty-one, I was selected to go to what was then Southern Rhodesia, on a Kelloggs sponsored exchange for six months. Now that was exciting! I had been club chairman and also secretary, in fact given my all. I don't know to this day why I was selected. I had actually applied for Canada but when I got to the area

---

1. A Young Farmers Club in the village of Roos in Holderness.

Sam at Young Farmers' stock judging event, 1955.

finals at York, there was a lad there who has since become a good friend, Jim Barton from Wetherby. Jim was, and is, an excellent self-presenter, a real natural and exudes confidence. He had actually arrived for the interview at the Station Hotel in York with a farm lorry, having delivered a load of beet to the factory. I thought that that in itself showed initiative, to park this ruddy great thing in the hotel car park, but that wasn't all. At the end of the day when we were about to leave, it was Jim who took home in his lorry a very attractive young girl who had also applied for an exchange visit, and whom we had all been eyeing up. I knew then I had no chance against him, but it was from the meeting that day that I was able to go forward to London and apply for Rhodesia. I am eternally grateful to the organisers for it was an experience of a lifetime.

I well remember the very first time I set foot on foreign soil. I must have been all of eighteen and I went with the local Young Farmers to Ostende in Belgium for ten days. We crossed from Dover to Ostende and as I walked down the gangplank, I hesitated at the bottom, with my foot poised, before I set it on foreign soil for the first time. I don't know what I expected, but I remember being disappointed because it didn't feel any different. Since then foreign travel has been a major part of my life and I believe I have now developed a real understanding of countries other than my own, they do indeed feel very different to me now. Whether it is the people, the buildings, the way of life, or the culture, I am not sure, but different they are.

My second job after leaving college was on a 300 acre farm in the village where my Mother went to live after her employer died. She had bought a house so I was able to live at home. Not sure whether that was a good thing or not. This particular farm had all of fifty sows, a flock of sheep and some cattle. We also grew potatoes. My primary role was to look after the livestock and help on the arable side as and when. Sows were simply run in a straw yard with a boar, and when they looked like pigging, we took them out into what was then purpose-built farrowing pens. These were literally loose boxes divided in two, with a block wall having a gap at the bottom to act as the creep area, and an infra-red lamp hanging behind it. Weaning at eight weeks was the norm and the pigs went into some of the old buildings. They were fed home mixed meal in round cast iron troughs upon which we poured water. The buildings were cold and uninsulated, and of course, hand mucking out was the norm. Straw was used in one corner to help against the cold floor.

What we did have though was a line of finisher pens built in a range of former wagon sheds. These were simply square block pens with a dunging passage, and at the front we had round metal bars above a salt glazed trough. Meal was put into a large round trough beneath a tap and then water was poured onto it where it was allowed to steep between feeds. The pigs always did well and had a sheen to their coats. I realised then that there was something in wet feeding. At that time, in the mid-1950s, most of the pigs were sold through local markets. Each village had its own butcher, so they would probably buy half-a-dozen pigs per week and bring them back to their own abattoir. There were one or two commercial factories about and sometimes pigs would go to Malton, the same factory which currently is the leading abattoir group in the country. I had occasion some time later, to spend seven years working for a farmer auctioneer, and some of the things the farmers would get up to in markets are almost unbelievable!

I enjoyed my time on that farm and at the end of three years it was time to take that once-in-a-lifetime trip to Southern Rhodesia, which today rejoices in the name of Zimbabwe. All I had to do was to get myself to London and thereafter, everything was taken care of and paid for. My local Young Farmers club gave me a donation of £90 that they hoped would cover my spending money and provide me with lots of films for photographs and slides, ensuring they would hear about the trip on my return. This I duly did and for the first ten years after my trip I was giving talks. I have the slides some forty years later and they are still in remarkable condition.

In 1957, Neville Thompson and I set out on our trip. Neville is now retired, having been a very successful farm manager here in the East Riding. He did a superb job and has won many awards for his contribution towards conservation and his farming ability. The estate he managed was immaculate. Neville was not from a farming background, his father was a mining engineer, so I think it is all the more credit to him. Like me, he too was working on a farm at the time of our trip. Prior to Rhodesia I had always assumed that farmer's sons would be selected.

At this point I would like to pay tribute to Barbara Tylden. At that time she was the International Secretary for the National Federation of Young Farmers Clubs. A nicer person you could not possibly wish to meet, she had a natural way with everybody, put everyone at ease and had the most amazing memory for faces and names. She knew personally everyone who had gone abroad on the exchange, likewise those who had visited our shores. If ever anyone deserved a mention in the Honours List, she should have been at the top. Sadly, Barbara passed away before the few of us who had thought of the honour could nominate her.

Before leaving Southampton on the *Stirling Castle*, a 25,000 tonne ocean-going liner, the longest time I had ever spent on a ship was a couple of hours crossing the Channel. I didn't know what to expect, or how I would pass the time. Someone had suggested that the Bay of Biscay would be rough and that we would suffer *mal de mer*. I need not have worried, the time passed so quickly and apart from a gentle swell when we hit the Capetown Rollers, it was a relatively smooth passage.

The ship had a lot of British passengers on board, who were either returning to work in various parts of Africa, or were going for the first time to take up employment in what was in those days, quite a lucrative venture. Africa was, and still is to some extent, an emerging nation. Farming was beginning to shift away from the native type of monoculture and I still believe, apart from the existing political ramifications, that with the sun and irrigation, there is more potential in Africa, than any other part of the world.

So what do you do on board for two weeks? It takes a couple of days to settle in and meet other passengers. The crew were very good, they organised some sort of entertainment every night and even we lowly lot in the bottom deck bunks had dinner with the Captain one evening. The ship had a swimming pool, there were deck games to play, exercising if you wished, reading rooms or deck chairs to relax in. Fortunately, there were quite a few of the opposite sex on board, which I must admit did help a bit. I had never seen flying fish before, or a school of porpoise. The ship called at Madeira for an afternoon, where we had the pleasure of not only having a quick look around this delightful island, but also sampling the free wine. As the ship approached Madeira we were met by a flotilla of rowing boats, which contained young children plus a host of things to buy, all locally crafted. The water was clear and you could easily discern the bottom of the sea. If you threw a coin into the water the children in the rowing boats would dive in to retrieve it. Many bargains were struck, the money was thrown down and the goodies were passed by rope back up to the ship. Not everyone wanted to go ashore. Neville and I did though, and I can distinctly remember as we scrambled on to a boat, looking down into the clear water where I could trace the lines of the ship, and was surprised to see how many barnacles were attached to it.

Every day there was a competition to see how far we had travelled in the last twenty-four hours. It was usually about 438 nautical miles. I did ask one of the crew exactly how far it was from leaving the quay at Southampton, to berthing in Cape Town? He told me it was 5,999 nautical miles and we would dock at precisely six o'clock in the morning in fourteen days time. The ship was run like clockwork, so it did not surprise me in the slightest when we bumped alongside in Cape

Town at exactly six as predicted. There were of course one or two highlights on the voyage. I well recall one night having a fancy dress parade. I will never know from where the passengers obtained their costumes, but there was quite an array. I have a slide that I sometimes show when giving a talk, which has nothing directly to do with pigs, but it does get the evening off to a flying start. One of the girls at the fancy dress parade had nothing more than a Union Jack wrapped round her. The Captain had been invited to judge the competition and as each competitor came forward, one of the ship's officers announced what they represented. Up till this point I had thought the captain to be a bit stiff and starchy and I believe it was his first command. When the flag girl came forward she simply said, 'Many a stiff battle has been fought under this flag'. Of course I will leave it to your imagination to decide who won, but at least it broke the ice for the captain who seemed to wear a permanent grin thereafter. At this point in my talk I relate to the audience that the slide reminds me of what a stiff battle we have in keeping pigs!

Cape Town from Table Mountain.

Table Mountain is a wondrous thing. We took the cable car up to the summit and spent some time there, before we left on the train for a three-day journey to Salisbury or Harare as it is now called. Looking down on the harbour, we could see the *Stirling Castle*; it looked quite small from that height. There was a bit of a haze over the Drakensburg mountains, alongside which the train track runs for a considerable distance, but there was no mistaking their beauty, truly magnificent. It was noticeable that in Cape Town as elsewhere in Africa we later discovered, all the streets run north and south while the avenues run east and west. At that time the Boers were not particularly friendly towards the English, as we found out firstly on the train and later when we were visiting farms in Rhodesia. When we arrived at farms where some Boers worked they would talk in Dutch. I thought that was most discourteous. The stewards on the train were all Boers and Neville and I were given the third sitting for meals, and we could never get any service or hot water, which meant shaving in cold water. I don't suppose air conditioning had been invented then, at least not on this train. It was hot and humid, along with red dust coming into our carriage all the time. It meant a clean shirt twice a day. As the railway is of slightly narrower gauge than ours, the train never really got up to a great speed. When we left Cape Town, we were at first drawn by an electric engine, but some time during that night it was changed to a coal-fired steamer. The driver must have been at the native brew, as he slammed into the train whilst reversing up to it, and caused us to fall out of our bunks.

Africa is beautiful but so varied. There are miles and miles of citrus groves, acres and acres of irrigated crops, followed by more miles of arid terrain. We had several short stops, one of which I remember was at a place called Dry Harts. It told us how high we were, how far from Cape Town and how far from Salisbury. Every time we stopped, there would be a collection of local people trying to sell their wares. One ruse we quickly cottoned on to was to lock our carriage door when we stopped, the reason being that when we were preoccupied leaning out of the train windows taking in the poverty and quaintness of the local people, some of them would creep round the other side of the train, enter your carriage, and pinch what they could lay their hands on.

The longest stop was at Kimberley, the famous diamond centre where the largest man-made hole in the world exists. After three days and two nights we eventually arrived in Salisbury, that beautiful wondrous city. Cecil Rhodes had the foresight to fully utilise the space available and thus, we found that all the streets were able to accommodate parking on both sides and yet leave enough room for a span of oxen to turn around. And for those of you who don't know there are twelve oxen in a span!

3 | Southern Rhodesia

I suppose Rhodesia warrants a book of its own, as it so rich in minerals and African tradition, but being landlocked is a disadvantage without doubt. Exporting meant either a long journey on what were little better than strip roads in those days (a feature of the Southern hemisphere), or a rail journey. Today, I believe flowers and fresh vegetables are flown out daily or at least were until the Mugabe regime took its toll.

The idea of the Young Farmers exchange visits were to exchange cultural ideas, see what made that particular country tick, live with the families, learn what you could and enjoy yourself into the bargain. I think both Neville and I achieved that. We actually stayed with thirty-three different families and visited over 100 farms, factories and sites. It was not uncommon to find in some of the valleys, like the Sabi, that three crops could be grown in a year. Vegetables simply grew as you looked at them. There were no sophisticated irrigation booms or reels, it was usually done by flood irrigation, a series of waterways which could be dammed and diverted, with a fall of 1 in 500. Labour of course was plentiful and cheap. Apartheid still reigned, but I never felt it was quite as intense there as perhaps in the Union of South Africa. The farmers looked after their labour very well and were housed and fed. The staff, or at least most of them, appreciated this fact greatly and were loyal in return. Each week a bullock was killed on most farms, just to feed the natives. They were also given mealie meal for porridge. Many of the men had more than one wife so each wife would have her own rondavel or roundhouse. To avoid poisoning or some other fate, no wife knew which house the husband was coming home to, and they had to taste the food first!

Education was not forgotten. On many a farm the farmer paid for a teacher for the children of the workers. I think it was recognised that it was necessary to educate them for the sake of future generations and a united country. It would also be to the employer's benefit to have people who could take on responsibility. I met several Rhodesian black people who spoke good English and were capable of acting as foremen on farms and doing a good job. It has to be said that they were the exception rather than the rule, and there was still an element of the white population who thought that all black people still had a mark on the base of their spines, where their tails had dropped off.

It was, I believe, widely accepted that as a race the black African population was at least 200 years behind us and that it would take several generations to bring them to equivalent status. Without doubt the African has a different approach to life. Tribal instincts are strong. Basically the men are lazy, they do the hunting for food while the women work the fields. Children are born - and die - with alarming regularity. More than once we saw a woman working in the fields with her hoe or badza as they are called, who would quietly go to the nearest stream, give birth, wash the baby in the river, throw it onto her back and then go back to work. She would then conceive again quite quickly. It was quite a knack getting the men to work on the farms. Success seemed to be assured if a good singer was employed and he was paid a bit extra. If the men were doing a repetitive manual job, they did it in time to the tempo of a song. The quicker the man sang, the faster they worked. Every house we stayed in had a cook boy, a washing boy, several gardener boys and maybe a maid. They were very well-fed and clothed and I believe they worshipped the ground their master walked on. Somehow it all seemed very acceptable. I suppose if the men had a downfall it was alcohol. They were allowed to brew their own beer on a Saturday night and quite literally they got well and truly stoned. It was while we were out there that a law was passed to allow blacks to buy the whites' beer. That caused a bit of a rumpus, but not many could afford it anyway.

Because of their drinking habits, it meant that many a time on a Monday morning the men were still hung over. Farmers were quick to cotton onto this and decided that Monday morning was the day when the meat for the week and the family was distributed. I think the wives then took charge and saw that their husbands were in attendance.

Another skill that some were very good and practiced at was forgetting. I well remember one morning a boy calling at the farmer's house to tell him that he had forgotten how to milk the cows! He wasn't kidding either as he had done it for six months without a problem. Another chap who wanted to knock off early for some reason stuck a pitchfork into a tractor tyre then told the boss it was busted and he couldn't do any more work. On another occasion, we were playing tennis with a family when one of their servants came and sat at the side of the courts. It wasn't until we finished that he spoke to the boss. He had been fighting and had a knife stuck in his ribs and thought the boss would help him in some way, but because he respected the boss he felt he could not disturb him until he had finished playing tennis! I thought that was taking loyalty a bit too far.

No doubt about it, in the late 1950s and early 1960s life for the white population in Rhodesia was idyllic. The men enjoyed a very high standard of living, they had superb houses, most with pools and tennis courts, their wives had an easy life, consisting of overseeing the running of the home and attending coffee mornings. The women were certainly well provided for by their husbands for if not, there was an abundance of bachelors who would gladly fulfil the role.

There was just about every sort of farming known to man in Rhodesia. We experienced ranching, pigs, sheep, cotton growing, bananas, avocados, paw paws, a vast range of other fruits and vegetables, herbage seed, pumpkins, tobacco and sugar cane, along with other produce like coffee, tea, maize, rubber, and a host of different forage crops. It appears that any mortal thing will grow there, which is why it breaks my heart to hear about how the white population is now being treated under the Mugabe regime. He is ruining what could be a superb economy based on agriculture.

Rhodesia (Zimbabwe) is a varied country, from the Chimanimani mountains in the Eastern Highlands, (Chimanimani means glistening, and they are glistening with minerals) to the ranching in the south and the fertile valleys of the midlands. At that time the country was divided into four main regions: Mashonaland, around Salisbury, Matabeleland around Bulawayo, Manicaland in the east, around Umtali, and Chipinga, all regions named after tribes, plus the midlands, which had such places as Fort Victoria, Queque, Gatouma and Gwelo.

There was immense rivalry between Salisbury and Bulawayo. The natives referred to Salisbury as Bombazonke, which means 'has everything', whilst Bulawayo had the name of Funazonke, which means 'has nothing and wants everything'. Actually I liked Bulawayo, it is a nice town.

We saw Lake McIlwain, the largest earth-walled dam in the Southern hemisphere, saw the beginnings of the now famous Kariba Dam, spent three days in the Wankie Game Reserve, and a day and two nights at the Victoria Falls – the latter something wondrous to behold. Whilst we were there, a couple of American tourists were talking to each other and one said, 'Gee bud, this makes Niagara look like a drop of sweat'. Having been to both I concur with him. Perhaps the other place that sticks out in my mind is where Cecil John Rhodes is buried. It is situated in the Matopos Hills, miles from anywhere. Apparently, he used to sit there surveying the surrounding beauty. He called it 'World's View'. It was his wish to be buried there and I can understand why. It is not only beautiful with all the mosses and the lichens on the surrounding rocks, but it is so perfectly peaceful.

I suppose visiting zoos and safari parks is a poor substitute for the real thing. We were fortunate when visiting the game reserve to go with one of the conservation officers, who was responsible for the bore holes which supplied the wild animals with their water. This meant we did not have to keep to the tourist trail and we spent many an hour way off the beaten track allowing us to see more wild life, lions in particular, than we would have seen as normal tourists. It is quite a sight to witness drinking time at the various watering holes. The animals drink in groups or species, one group standing back whilst

Typical farmhouse with Chimanimani Mountains in the background.

another took their fill. One of the funniest things to witness is a giraffe trying to get down to drink. As their mouths are a long way from the ground they gently spread their front legs till they are almost horizontal, a sort of front leg splits. Often, just as they were nearly all the way down something would frighten them, and they would instantly straighten up. This all took time and it was quite common for the whole process to take half-an-hour before a giraffe was able to drink.

Not all wild life lives in the reserves. Hippos and rhinos are quite common in the local rivers along with crocodiles. On one ranch we were shown the bones of some cattle lying in the river bed. Apparently if a croc gets hungry, he will lie in wait until a bullock or cow comes for a drink. As they are drinking, they are obviously sloping down hill and can't back away, so when a croc grabs them by the nose, then they are simply pulled into the water to drown.

Snakes are one of my pet hates. There is an abundance of them in Africa. One night on our return to our rondavel we found a large snake curled up in the middle of my bed. The

Lioness in the Wankie Game Reserve, 1957.

farmer didn't hesitate he simply shot it with a 12 bore and ruined the bedspread into the bargain! Another farm where pigs were kept, had a bit of a problem with snakes, they would eat the young piglets and one day we found a snake fast asleep on top of the corrugated iron roof, with eleven bulges in its stomach, an entire litter. I suppose like rats, if a snake can escape then it will. If you surprise or frighten it and it can't escape, well, that is another story.

We are lucky here in Britain that we don't have too many nasties, like scorpions for example. Neville and I were picnicking one day by the side of a river under some trees with a family, when a scorpion dropped out of a tree and actually fell down the front of Neville's shirt where it stung him. Though doctors and hospitals were few and far between most families they kept anti-serums of various sorts around the house. When our host saw what had happened, he bundled everyone into the truck and drove at breakneck speed back to his house, so that Neville could have treatment. We were a considerable distance from the house and on the way back he didn't stop to open the gates on the ranch, he simply drove straight through them, it was that urgent. Needless to say, Neville was a bit groggy for a couple of days.

Although everyone worked hard they knew how to relax. It gets dark most of the year around about six o'clock in the evening. Everyone sat on their veranda and had a drink of beer, referred to as 'sundowner' time. I felt this was all very civilised. They were great ones for their radios and knew all the latest hits. If I remember rightly, it was around that time the song *A White Sports Coat and a Pink Carnation* was released and for days after it was on every lip.

The first farm we stayed at was at Bindura with Leslie Mossop. It was a real education. He lived quite frugally and had

Sam on horse in Southern Rhodesia.

the most amazing farm covered in small hills he could drive
up, and from which to survey the wondrous vista before his
eyes. That was all he wanted from life, that and his radio which
was driven by a spare battery from his pick-up truck. When the
battery ran down he took the charged up one from his pick-
up, put it on the radio and the flat battery was then put on the
truck, which would be taken down the hill outside his house to
'jump start', and then the truck would charge that one up too.
It was on Leslie's farm at Bindura that we experienced our first
rain storm and it helped me understand the problems they had
trying to keep roads passable. The non-metalled roads quickly
develop corrugations and are graded a couple of times a year
to level them out. The trick about driving on them was to get
up enough speed so that your wheels only touched the top of
the corrugations otherwise it was a bit of a hazard and very
uncomfortable.

I had never seen cattle dipped before. They were dipped
once a week in summer and once every two weeks in winter.

Ticks were the problem and if not done all sorts of diseases and conditions would surely strike. I seem to recall that Blackleg was one of them. It wasn't a problem to dip the cattle, they were quite used to it and I suppose a cooling dip in a hot climate is quite refreshing. They ran down the race and took the plunge effortlessly. It was hot, very, but it was a dry heat, which is always more tolerable than a humid heat.

Another character with whom we stayed was Ben Barry, who gave us a superb time. He had been given five years to live ten years previously and he lived life to the full. What his problem had been I know not, but you would never guess anything had been wrong with him. He was a superb farmer, known the length and breadth of Rhodesia, kept a dozen mongrel dogs, which took it in turns for one pack to go baboon and leopard hunting, while the other pack came home to lick their wounds and recuperate before going off again.

He employed a big game hunter to take Neville and I leopard shooting and of course we had many a day hunting baboons, which are a plague. They ruin maize crops by pulling off the cobs, tucking them under their arms, and then when they pick the next cob, the first one drops out. So it was quite common for them to go down a row, pull all the cobs and at the end of their foraging have only one cob under their arms! Quite often on farms baboon hunters were employed and paid a few pence per head killed. Ben was taking us to a dinner one night and thought he had better put on a clean shirt only to find when he went to the cupboard that a cat had had a litter of kittens on it. A year after we had been over there, I was informed that Ben had met a nice lady and settled down and eventually fathered three daughters.

Boss Lilford was probably the largest farmer in Rhodesia. He was the force behind Ian Smith who was Prime Minister for a time. Boss Lilford not only farmed extensively, but he had interests in hotels, gold mines, race horses, fishing lakes, so many things. At the end of our tour we had a free week and we went back to his ranch. He was the first man to introduce Santa Gertrudis cattle to Africa, from the King Ranch in Texas. That breed is five-eighths Shorthorn and three-eighths Bramham. They were wonderful range animals with phenomenal growth rates. Apparently the strain Boss bought was from a particularly good bull called Monkey.

The indigenous cattle did well in the scrub conditions. Pure-bred Herefords or Angus from Europe suffered from tropical degeneration if bred pure. Having said that, they were ideal for crossing on the native cattle like the Tulli when the offspring were fed semi-intensively. There were actually a couple of well established Hereford and Angus herds in Rhodesia, but the breeders needed to return to Britain for replacements fairly often as these breeds had to be managed completely differently, which usually meant more expensively.

Neville Thompson and Sam driving a mule cart.

Women carrying various loads on their heads.

In the designated indigenous reserves of which there were quite a few, it was very noticeable how thin the cattle were. The land was overstocked, overgrazed, cattle not dipped or wormed for the simple reason that they were the means of raising a dowry. You would sell one of your daughters for maybe three or four cattle, which would then enable you to go and buy another wife to have more daughters and so on. Maybe that is a slight exaggeration, but there was an element of truth in it. Talking about daughters and wives, it is amazing how the womenfolk carry things on their heads, sometimes piled up quite high but they have a superb sense of balance.

Both Neville and I were offered jobs while we were out there. We talked about it a lot and decided to ask Boss Lilford for his advice. He told us that we would be fine for a while although he did not know for how long, but he was sure that one day the whites would have their throats cut. About ten years ago I saw on the front of one of the Sunday papers, that Boss had indeed been murdered, shot outside his house which by then had become a fortress with security fencing.

The Young Farmers of Rhodesia were indeed very keen. Whereas our YF motto is, 'Good Farmers, Good Countrymen, Good Citizens', their motto was 'Better Farmers, Better Countrymen and Better Citizens'. Some of them still keep in touch. Some are now living in Britain others have immigrated to South Africa. Many are in danger of having their farms taken from them, most fear for their futures, even their lives at times. It seems such a pity, such a waste, such a wonderful country. Will men never learn to live together?

It was while I was there that I had my first flight in an airplane. It was an old Dakota, due to fly from Bulawayo to Salisbury early one morning. We boarded, the engines started up and we set off down the runway, only to find one of the engines had caught fire! That was not a very comforting experience.

It is surprising how fast time goes - April to August seemed to pass in a flash. We had been due to fly back via Angola, calling at Elizabethville and Brazaville, but uprisings were taking place. It was the beginnings of the troubles in Angola. We did not know this until we arrived at Salisbury airport very early

Dakota DC3: Sam's first ever flight.

one morning. We were told we could either wait another day or two or we could if we liked, go on a brand new Viscount, which was leaving at eight o'clock, to drop crews off en route to England. The plane was also going to be fitted with radar. Having spent so much time in the bush and on isolated properties, where we had virtually forgotten what the female form was like (well not quite) we didn't have to think very long to decide that it would indeed be nice to fly with a planeload of air stewardesses.

I would think these days that Harare could be reached by plane in maybe nine or ten hours. It took us three days and two nights to land back at Heathrow. It was nonetheless an extremely interesting flight. We landed firstly at Ndola, which was in Northern Rhodesia, now Zambia, followed by Entebbe at the top of Lake Victoria in Uganda. Here the plane was fumigated against tsetse fly. Our next stop consisted of having a meal in Khartoum airport. We were a bit apprehensive and were advised only to drink proprietary brands of water, out of a bottle. The waiters were an odd looking bunch, they had scars on their faces and several had lethal looking swords dangling at their waists. I have no idea what the meat was, probably camel. All I can remember was being pleased to get back onto the plane. Those of you who are good at geography will know that Khartoum is where the Blue Nile and the White Nile meet. As we came into land it was a spectacular sight to see the two rivers meandering to become one and just before we landed, as dusk approached, all the lights in the town came on. I really do have vivid memories of this. From there it necessitated a further few hours in the dark to a place on the Nile called Wadi Halfa. The airport was just a strip in the desert, probably five miles from anywhere. On the airstrip there was an unusual plane with a camera in the nose. We discovered that it belonged to

Twentieth Century Fox, the film studio, who were shooting a film in the desert. We assumed, when we eventually got to the hotel that it must be full of film stars, as we had to doss down in the annexe. Apparently, if ever the annexe became full you had to go onto a rat-infested boat on the adjacent river, where if you fell into the water you needed seven different injections when you came out - if you came out!

We had driven from the airport such as it was, in a rickety old bus over sand dunes, past a few camp sites where the locals were sleeping outdoors next to their camels. What few houses there were consisted of square huts made from either mud or camel dung. It was extremely hot in our rooms. We had to put something on our feet to stop the heat from the stone floor, and wear our pyjamas to keep the hot air from our bodies, despite a large propeller type fan constantly going round. I think all it was actually doing was warming up the air!

I distinctly remember next day at breakfast we had a plate of Kellogg's corn flakes, which as we were being sponsored by them, I thought very fitting. I don't suppose I will ever return to Wadi Halfa, although it would probably be interesting to see how things have changed, if indeed they have.

Bengazi in Libya was the first port of call the next day and as we landed on the runway a camel came strolling towards the plane and whose wing passed over the top of it. When we stopped I said to the Captain, 'That was a close thing!' at which he just laughed and replied, 'It always does that, every time'.

I had never flown over the Mediterranean before, which we did on our way to Rome, also flying over Mount Etna in Sicily, which was smoking and erupted the very next day. We needed to spend the rest of that day and night in Rome. It was, and still is, a bustling city. We hired a taxi to take us to the Coliseum and other sights of interest and paid the driver with

Rhodesian cigarettes. There are so many things to see and do in Rome that I must return again one day.

Viscounts didn't fly at any great height, so the flight over the Alps was brilliant. We just seemed to skim the snow-clad mountain tops, affording us the most magnificent view. Landing at Heathrow, where the Queen's Building had just been opened, seemed like a grass field, relevant to what it is today. Our respective families were waiting for us and as usual wanted to know everything immediately. I, however, am still remembering my time in Rhodesia nearly fifty years later.

4 | Markets

Upon my return from that fabulous trip, the next few years were indeed very hectic. It had been my intention to return to my old job but when I arrived home, a job offer was waiting with a local farmer who was also a brilliant auctioneer. He wanted a sort of right-hand man. I spent seven years with Eric. Shortly after I joined him, the neighbouring farm came on the market, which he bought, giving us then 300 acres to farm. I then moved into the farmhouse as a bachelor, which meant furnishing the place and stocking it with the various items, which seemed to be so necessary.

Every Monday we went to Hull cattle market, which was for prime fat stock but with a store pig section also, and on Wednesday we drove to Beverley for store stock sales. Believe it or not there were seven different firms of agricultural auctioneers and valuers in each of the markets. That meant we had to take it in turns to sell. One week in seven we had first turn when you would expect to sell most of the stock, but there was never any week when you had nothing to sell, as there were the three sections, cattle, sheep and beef. After the first auctioneer started, half-an-hour later number two could crack off, then we all followed on in turn. It all seemed very civilised even if there was fierce competition. One of the firms was the family with whom we lived in the threshing days. They were quite a large firm and had lots of farm sales. Most of the auctioneers had farms and would sell all their stock through the markets bringing stock of some sort each week. We were no exception. Eric bought me a Land Rover (one of the first diesels) and a livestock trailer. He would leave at eight o'clock in the morning to go to market whilst I attended to the stock, set the men on at the farm, then I would load up either some pigs or cattle or sheep in season to take with me. Being a farmer and an auctioneer had some advantages. It was as Eric called it a 'good Jack and a Jill.' Eric specialised in selling pigs and often we sold 2,000 or more in one day, particularly stores when Beverley was the leading pig market. If Eric got over-enthusiastic and popped in the odd bid and was landed with a packet of animals, I was there with the trailer and would simply take them home. Try doing that today, there would be so many rules and regulations.

It was common in those days to 'tout' for business when the various farmers pulled up with their trailers or as the lorries arrived. It often proved an interesting exercise. If we had a first turn coming up, I would sometimes spend an afternoon or two during the week, going around various farms seeking entries for the next week. I suppose in those seven years I got to know most of the farmers in the area, and perhaps more importantly, some of their daughters!

I remember once being invited to visit one of our customers who always sent us his pigs to market. He had somehow bred a litter of fourteen outstanding pigs and had sent the castrates to the factory. The grading sheet had shown they were the longest pigs the factory had ever had in. Our customer felt the gilts were too good to go to slaughter and would we be interested in having a look at them? I called in, liked what I saw, gave him £1 more than the slaughter pigs had averaged, had a cup of tea and arranged a date with his daughter for that evening – all-in-all a very successful day! I brought the pigs back with me and as true as I sit here, those six gilts never had less then sixteen pigs until they had produced six litters. They were unbelievable. If only I had had the foresight then to make more of them, they would have been the basis of a breeding pyramid, but in those days, most things were pedigree or pure and they were Landrace cross Large White.

The 1950s and 1960s doubtless saw the heyday of the markets. There are of course some diehards who will continue to sell their stock through the marts so long as they exist. But it was also once a social occasion where it was customary for farmers attending the market to bring their wives into town to do some shopping. Nowadays, wives are more independent and go to town anyway, and why not?

There were lots of tricks in the trade in those days. One of the simplest was to fill the pigs' bellies up with feed prior to coming to market, so that they weighed better. One farmer was notorious for standing at the weighbridge when his pigs were coming through and gently press his foot on the scale to gain a bit of extra weight. I have also seen attempts made to 'tip' the man in charge of weighing so that he would write down a heavier weight. Nobody ever wanted their stock sold first, no matter if they came in first. That could create problems, but as we always had stock going in we could use the first pen, and if the price didn't reach what was expected, the stock would simply be moved to another pen and tried again a bit later. There is always more than one way of killing a dog than choking it with pudding!

Long before the supermarkets became so popular, there were plenty of buyers and often bidding was quite brisk. The buyers would occasionally decide to form a 'ring' in order to keep prices down, and by not bidding against each other they ensured they had the pick of what they wanted. When this happened a good auctioneer came into his own by knowing the value of the stock and more or less taking them to that value. For example, if Eric came unstuck, we could either take them home, or he had a couple of pals who would take them off his hands.

Prime stock was graded by an official Ministry grader who

would put the appropriate mark on them, thus ensuring the correct subsidy or make up payment was obtained. If cattle were not sufficiently well finished, they would be rejected. Grading caused a lot of controversy. Naturally, every farmer thought his cattle were the best and deserved top grade. Some buyers were astute enough to buy the rejects and have them killed hoping to get them graded deadweight, which often happened, for it isn't always the best cattle that make the farmer the most money. This fact was brought home to me time and time again. Yes, farmers love to have nice looking cattle with good conformation when finished, and they would probably make more per hundredweight than lesser mortals, but invariably the better cattle cost a lot more money as stores when they were purchased. However, buyers are not daft. They knew what the weight of the pigs should be so would pay that bit less per score for them. They could easily check the killing out percentage and would naturally pay a bit more for those that did better. Very often the same buyer would buy the stock from an individual farmer on a regular basis if he liked what he was getting. So, I always thought it was better to be honest and do a good job rather than take short cuts.

I thoroughly enjoyed the markets. They were long days and then there was the stock on the farm to see to when returned. My own personal feelings today about markets is that they are fine for store sheep and cattle, maybe some finished animals, but pigs, well, I think they should go direct to an abattoir. The modern pig is not designed to be loaded, unloaded, put in pens in a market, knocked about with sticks or prods by a drover, loaded up again and probably mixed with other pigs then transported to wherever. So far as store pigs go, it was deemed quite acceptable then to have hundred people bringing a run of stores into a market, being penned next to each

Combing koga: spring wheat – old Massey Harris combine.

other, and I must admit, it was not often there was any disease trouble. We didn't seem to have any disease problems then, at least not the conditions we find in some animals now. Pigs were certainly hardier and there was always the odd dealer on whom we would take a gamble on a run of pigs, even if they didn't look quite right. Sometimes two buyers would fall out and then prices would rocket. I learned a lot during my time in the markets. If on my travels I saw some stock, which a farmer was prepared to do a deal on, Eric allowed me to buy them and when they went to market, if they got profit, he always took a share but likewise if they lost – as a result you learnt very quickly.

I suppose people prefer to have quality stock and generally in the long run it pays off. However, I well remember bidding for an Ayrshire bullock in the market, which cost the princely sum of £36.00. I don't know why I did because it was entirely the wrong shape and a bit pot-bellied but there was just something about it, which I liked. I took it back to the farm, yarded it, and fed it on stockfeed potatoes and very little else, and within a couple of months it doubled in value, it simply piled on weight. Another time I bought a Belted Galloway, not known for their quick growth. It was sort of nearly finished or so I thought, but it turned out to be more hair than meat. It weighed 7cwts and cost £9.00 per cwt, equalling £63.00. We had the damned thing for nearly a year and when it was sold, it weighed 9cwts and made £7.00 per cwt, equalling £63.00! I never bought another. It is somewhat sobering to look back at the prices for stock and other farm produce during this era. Barley was about £17.00 per tonne and weaners would fetch maybe £5.00 if you were lucky. A good lamb would make £7.00 or £8.00 a head.

My former boss, Eric Wright, in a crop of Blenda spring oats, 1960.

On the farm, which was good boulder clay, a typical Holderness soil, we grew wheat, barley, oats, turnips, mangolds, red clover, sometimes beans and occasionally tares. Peas became quite popular and before the days of direct combining, we would cut them with a grass reaper and they would be turned by hand and put on tri-pods to dry. That, of course, was after the introduction of the Ferguson tractor, because that would handle a buckrake, which in turn carried the tri-pods up to either the threshing machine or the stack. Peas were handled like eggs. Silage began to appear, again because of the Fergy and the buckrake. Farming changed rapidly. Our binder was put in a shed never to reappear and we had a Massey 726 combine. Gone was the stooking, the leading, the stacking, the threshing and of course the chaff carrying. The corn was still then bagged up on the combine. Our particular one had a chute down which bags were slid once tied. We tried to leave them in

a row so that when we came down later with the Reffold sack elevator, which entailed some skilful driving, we could actually pick up the sacks and drop them onto the back of the man on the trailer, when they would then be put in the granary or on a shed floor for later disposal.

The Reffold elevator was an ingenious piece of equipment, the drawbar at the front was offset to pick up bags, and when you wanted to tow it home or to another field, the drawbar was then fitted onto the elevator at the other end and towed backwards, either behind the tractor or behind the trailer. The small jockey wheels were lifted off the ground when picking up bags and dropped by lever when going on the road. Travelling with the elevator on the road was just a steady job as the jockey wheels would get 'wobble' if you went too fast which did one of two things, it either meant that the elevator wandered about, or it could tear the tyres off the wheels.

Baling clover at Flinton. Fordson tractor on the left, Allis Chalmers on the right.

Red clover we grew as a break crop. Sometimes we baled it and sold it, often for as little as £7.00 per tonne. We were never going to get fat on that, but you could grow two tonnes of wheat per acre after it. Other times we would stack it and use it ourselves. Sheep certainly liked it as indeed they did the white clover in our leys. We never grew successive wheat crops, it was unheard of.

The seeds mixture with clover that we used for the sheep was always plastered with manure from the cattle yards. No artificial fertiliser was deemed necessary. One of the problems we had in those days was that we had insufficient horsepower to sow the farm in the autumn, one reason why there was a predominance of spring sowing. Busting up grass and clover leys was sometimes done by a contractor using an old steam engine drag, converted to go behind a Fowler crawler tractor. That was fine, made an excellent job, but we had nothing with which to break the lumps of soil down. If it rained sufficiently by the end of September or into October, we could just about manage to plough the leys that had been paddled solid by the sheep. Crops did not seem to get any diseases. Arguably, it was the same for them as for the livestock inasmuch as we did not push them as hard as we need to do today, so they were never stressed.

Drainage became recognised as one of the ways forward, so several companies were set up in our area, using second hand Buckeye machines from America. We had several fields drained to great effect. Yields improved along with soil structure. Grants began to materialise for farm improvements, including buildings. Sheds appeared in the area, concrete yards, shed floors even some roadways were becoming quite commonplace, farming began to look prosperous. Farmers responded in like manner and I believe I was fortunate to be farming in an area, which still even now ranks as one of the better-farmed parts of the country.

Pigs began to appear as a serious part of the farming scene, instead of a hitherto back-yard industry. Most farms had wooden huts in the fields for farrowing, which were simply pulled on once a week. Gradually farrowing crates took over and the wooden huts disappeared. Brian Thomas emerged as a front-runner in the pig building sector, many of his houses are still with us today. Intensive pigs were something new and brought their own problems.

It took some time before the traditional farm buildings were altered to try and take account of modern methods. During my time with Eric, even though I say it myself, I worked very hard, very long hours. I was never paid an hour of overtime, but I did get 10% of the profits as a bonus, so there was incentive. I remember we had an old Bamford tractor-driven plate mill and roller, which was used for grinding the corn for the pigs, the sheep, and the cattle, before we installed a new Reffolf mixer and an Essex hammer mill. We had three Fordson Super Major tractors, one of which had a pulley drive on. After the men had finished with them during the day, I used to set this tractor up to the mill and spend a couple of hours grinding twice a week. I didn't mind at all, and at one time all the rations were mixed by shovel on the meal house floor. Lambing time was always a bit hairy, only me to do it really, so, I often went a bit short on sleep. Never mind, it was all great experience and being young and quite fit I suppose, I thoroughly enjoyed my life. I made time to go out, although sometimes if I had to pick up a girlfriend, I was often a bit behind time. I continued in Young Farmers until I had to come out at twenty-six. I became club leader for a while, and then a member of the advisory panel.

5 | Life in Lincolnshire

Having by this time attained the ripe old age of twenty-nine, and just married for the first time, I felt that perhaps it was time for a move, but the carrot that had been dangled in front of me for some time, always just seemed to be that bit out of reach.

Anyone who has been taught the art of working Holderness land,[1] I believe should be able to work any kind of land, particularly as we had no powered implements like a power harrow then. The frost was relied on quite heavily to break down the ploughing, hence another reason for spring time drilling. Up until this time we had relied on discs and rolls to break up the lumps, before trying to finalise the seed bed with chisel harrows or duck foots as they were called in Lincolnshire. I believe everyone who is into arable farming should spend some time in Lincolnshire. An interesting and challenging post was advertised in the *Farmers Weekly*, for a personal assistant on a 750 acre farm in South Lincolnshire. I felt this was perhaps the sort of job to motivate me, something totally different. I moved there in 1964. The farm was diverse not only in soil type but also cropping. I had never had experience of growing blackcurrants before and we grew 20 acres on contract for Ribena. The farm carried 90 cows, grew sugar beet and sugar beet for seed, potatoes, cereals, oil seed rape, daffodil bulbs and rhubarb, wild oats, couch grass and black grass!

Eric was not amused when I told him I was leaving and for a couple of years we had no contact. Some five years later when I came back to Beverley, Eric, although not retired, had bought a house in Beverley only 100 yards away from where I was to live. We took up again from where we had left off and

---

1. Holderness is an area of strong boulder clay. Holderness runs from Bridlington to Spurn Point the Humber Estuary, and from Hull to Beverley across to Bridlington, almost half the East Riding.

he remained a very good friend and still a mentor until his sad death a quarter of a century later.

My move to Lincolnshire was to a typical Fen farm. The house where I lived was two-and-a-half miles down a dead end fen road, completely isolated, and we actually had a generator for electricity, although there was obviously a phone and the inevitable Aga cooker. I didn't mind the isolation, but in life we have to have some thoughts for 'her indoors'. This, I fear, I neglected to do, I was too engrossed in what I was doing to notice the tell-tale signs, so it was hardly surprising when I came home for tea one night to find that my wife had 'upsticks and gone'!

The five years I spent in Lincolnshire added considerably to my experience. Harry, like Eric before him, was a first class mentor and remains a close friend to this day. It was about this time in farming that crop walkers began to appear or crop consultants as they are now called. Carbyne had been developed by Fisons for the control of wild oats and for a time it was very successful. No one could tell me why there were so many wild oats in the area. The farm I lived on had just been put to Harry's original farm and I suppose the old boy who had farmed it previously had let things slip a bit. The chemical companies were expanding, bringing out new treatments for the plethora of weeds we seemed to grow, and would send representatives out to walk the crops and advise about treatment. We used Chafers [2] at the time, as we hired a sprayer from them, and I remember also using liquid fertiliser. There was a time when they had a range of weed killers, which could also be applied in liquid fertiliser. It was a developing time in farming, anhydrous ammonia was developed which we injected with excellent results even though it did tear up some wheat plants. Rotary mowers were a godsend far superior to the old cutter bar

2. Family firm and leaders in liquid fertilisers and sprays.

type, and prilled mono-germ sugar beet seed meant we could use precision drilling, which saved a lot on the laborious task of hand hoeing, particularly when used in conjunction with band spraying.

An Alvan Blanch drier was installed to replace the previous smaller model in order to cope with the extra acreage. The cows were milked through a bail, which was taken down the fen during the summer months, where we could utilise more of the land and then taken up to the main farm in winter, where it operated like a parlour. It actually worked well except when it was down the fen, it operated from a petrol engine, in fact we had a couple of spares as well, but sometimes they would not start. We had a gas conversion for them, which I believe made them quieter, but starting remained a problem. I remember we had one herdsman who started at four in the morning. I think he was absolutely mad and I would hear him come past my house at around three-thirty and I would wonder if he would come back later saying he had problems. It would take more than the fingers of both hands to cover the amount of times I was knocked up to help him start the damned engines. I had the engines stripped down, they were de-coked, everything was as it should be and I never did get to the bottom of what the problem was. Perhaps some engines are like some women, a bit temperamental?

Life in Lincolnshire was totally different from life in Yorkshire. I suppose I missed the rolling countryside and the glorious Wolds. It was so flat in Billingborough that although Boston was eighteen miles away, you could clearly see Boston Stump. The men were also different. Some of the jobs were undertaken on piecework, which to me was a bloody nightmare. Sugar beet hoeing and singling was one such task and the men who applied the fertiliser were paid so much an acre extra, the same for spraying. I remember that all the men, and we had ten at first, all lived in cottages just outside the entrance to where Harry lived in the village. In the morning they would stand outside the gates until the clock finished striking seven, then shuffle in, stand in the first shed and await their orders. I had been there since six forty-five, having driven the two-and-a-half miles, and having had a word with the cowman, before the men appeared. The funny thing was that as soon as I had told the first man what I wanted him to do, instead of getting on with it straightaway, he would stand and listen to what the others were going to do! In fact the whole lot stood there, mulling it over in their minds. I found the whole attitude frustrating. It was as if they had been singled out for the less favourable tasks.

This practice of standing outside the gates used to infuriate me and I mentioned it to Harry one day, who fully understood but said it was custom, they had always done it and he more or less just accepted it. However, it was a different story at four in the afternoon when it was knocking off time, they would be streaming through the gate as the clock was striking! One day I locked the gates and waited until the clock had finished. Their comments were that I was 'A bloody Yorkshire slave driver', but at least I had made my point.

If you want to see human nature in its true form, invite casual labour to pick blackcurrants! For three weeks each year it gave me a permanent thumping headache. We opened at seven in the morning, the ladies from the village would start to trickle in and it was a constant battle to make sure they completely cleared a bush, before moving on. It was obviously easier to pick the bigger ones and the ones more visible, than to open a bush and 'find' the fruit that was concealed. If a new picker arrived and you asked them to finish a particular patch, they would probably curse as only women can and say that they hadn't come to do 'odding', which meant clearing up behind the others. They were, of course, paid by weight of fruit picked. They would present themselves at the weigher with a bucket of currants and would receive a ticket in exchange, which was duly exchanged for cash when they went home. Of course, some tried to disfigure the tickets to make the amount more, if for example they only had part of a bucket. Others would put stones in the bottom of their buckets, in the hope that we wouldn't know who had done it when we transferred the currants to the trays for despatch. One day I caught a youth who had popped down to the stream at the end of the field and had put water and gravel in his bucket first!

I can laugh about it now but it was hard going at the time. Our neighbours were one of the first to have a currant-picking machine. They grew over 100 acres though. The problem with machines was that the whole of the bush was cut down. This in turn meant bushes couldn't be pruned properly, resulting in too much new growth and harvesting every other year. There was in fact the choice of a self-propelled machine, or a static to which the entire branches could be brought. We persevered with hand labour. Frost damage was also a possibility. We had irrigation set up so if there was a frost warning, we could spray water onto the currants, or at least to those areas which were vulnerable at the time. Originally I thought how could watering a susceptible plant keep frost off? The answer, of course, is quite simple for water is above freezing point. It was possible to take out frost insurance. Harry reckoned one year that he ought to do that, as he had gone so many years without any trouble. He was absolutely right as we got frozen off more or less completely. We were paid out, but the premium then onwards was exhorbitant, watering was definitely the cheaper option.

I found sugar beet seed a fascinating crop to grow. We drilled two wide rows of barley, interspaced with one row of sugar beet. The barley was combined as normal, giving maybe better than half a yield, and the beet for seed was left to mature the following year.

I made many friends whilst in Lincolnshire, all in the industry and they still keep in touch. Harry has now retired but still takes a keen interest in what is going on. I suppose once a farmer, always a farmer.

I didn't bother much about holidays, although when I first arrived Harry said to me, 'I expect when we are busy, you will want to be here, but in quieter times, just take yourself off for the day'. I thought that was not only good advice, but it gave me a message at the same time. However, I did take a week off in 1969, when I stayed with an uncle who farmed in Alston, in Cumbria. Life up there is again totally different. Uncle Laurie was a real character and as tough as old boots. He was then in his late eighties and as active as a cricket. It was an enjoyable week, just walking up the fell every morning and chatting about farming in general, and the family, how the various members came to be on which farm and into which farming family they had married.

Many were the times I saw him come in soaked to the skin. He would stand with his back to the fire with steam rising from him. He would have a cup of coffee and then go out to milk the cows! Even at that age, I had a job keeping up with him as he pounded the fells, he would simply say, 'Come on now, come on!' He had some marvellous expressions and I well remember asking him one morning if I needed to take a coat with me to the fell? He simply replied, 'When it's fine, take a coat, when it's raining, please yourself!'

I can only ever remember him being ill once. He had constipation. The family had sent for the doctor, who administered pills. Uncle Laurie had never, ever met the doctor and I reckon the doctor would never have met anyone quite like him! The pills were put in the fire. He had all his life drunk the water in the puddles on the fell. The water was reddish coloured from the ochre in the peaty soil and I guess more than a bit of sheep dung too. Having been confined to the house which had annoyed him intensely, he decided he would struggle up the fell the next day and drink of his beloved water as he said it would cure anything. I asked him if it had worked. He smiled and said, 'Aye, I shit half a bucket full!'

On the way back to Lincolnshire from Alston, I called to see my mother. On the way I passed a farm at Beverley where the pea viners were at work, and were a bit bogged down. I knew the farm and I knew they had a large Jersey herd. What I did not know then was that I would be back at that farm two days later for an interview.

Back in Lincolnshire I called to see Harry for an update and he told me that John Sobey from Lugg & Gould, the management consultants, had been on the phone for me. I had met John at a management course at Stoneleigh [3] the previous year. I rang him and he said that he wanted me to go for an interview the next day at Beverley, to take on the role of manager for the four farms that I had passed only the previous day. I immediately went to see Harry who told me I had his blessing, would be sorry if I went, but he would not stand in my way. But if I was successful as he felt sure I would be, he would like me to stay to see harvest over. I drove up to Beverley the following morning full of apprehension.

---

3. The National Agricultural Centre at Stoneleigh Park in Warwickshire.

6 | Back to East Yorkshire

The journey in those days from South Lincolnshire took a bit longer than it does today. There was no Humber Bridge to cross, there was either the option of cutting across to the A1 and travelling up via Doncaster, or motoring up through the wonderful farming county of North Lincolnshire and crossing the Humber on one of the three paddle steamer ferries, which plied their trade between Corporation Pier in Hull and Barton-on-Humber on the south bank. These were super old ships and took between twenty and forty-five minutes to cross, depending entirely on the tide, as the Humber is full of sand banks. It was quite exciting I suppose on looking back, as at Hull you drove down a gangway to a floating pontoon, and at the other side, once you had negotiated the gangway, you had to drive along a railway platform which was not very wide. On board there was even a first class saloon, whilst we peasants had a choice of either a bar or a café. I was interested in the engines. They were totally immaculate, even the massive conrods that slowly went backwards and forwards, driving what seemed to be at a very slow pace, were brightly polished. There was always a man with an enormous shovel, facing what seemed like a mountain of coal, swiftly transferring it into what appeared to be a bottomless pit, through the fire door. That must have been one of the hardest jobs a man could have, perhaps even worse than threshing.

Those three ferries have now gone to new homes. There was the *Lincoln Castle*, the *Wingfield Castle* and the *Tattershall Castle*. Visitors to the Thames Embankment can see one of them, the *Tattershall*, which is now a restaurant and hardly recognisable as the same ship. Gone are the engines and of course it has been completely altered inside. I had a meal on some time ago and it brought back many memories. The East Riding Young Farmers were always leaders in their field and good at coming up with ideas. For several years we had what we called a 'Riverboat Shuffle'. This meant we hired one of the ferries for the evening and sailed down to Spurn Point. That took at least one-and-a-half hours each way and I can recall that we were cheering on the stoker that night to keep his shovel going! It was quite good fun, dancing on the decks of the ferry, and even time for a bit of romance too. Having said that, I believe the Young Farmers were good at finding places for romance generally.

I arrived ten minutes early for the interview. I was quite unprepared, I had never had a professional job interview before and wasn't sure what sort of questions I might be asked and how detailed the questions might be. The owner was a real gentleman, who lived in a magnificent private residence, five miles away from the four farms, which bordered the whole of the north of Beverley and a stretch east also. Lugg & Gould had been called in to act as Management Consultants on the farms. I had actually seen the job advertised some six months prior and had thought at the time that I would not envy the chap who took that job. The family were very successful in the fishing industry, with a fleet of deep-sea trawlers, some seventeen, at the time I went there in 1969. Very wisely over the years, they had invested in land, and in time, they acquired four farms which all joined, more or less in a line and more or less 250 acres each. It had been run by a foreman and perhaps a succession of managers over a period of maybe some twenty-five years and as the acreage grew it had been deemed necessary to alter the structure quite substantially. I think I can safely say that the farms were in a mess, physically and financially. The interview lasted all day, with a break for lunch in the Beverley Arms Hotel. I asked why the position had not been

filled before now and John Sobey to his credit admitted that
they had interviewed a number of applicants who had either
been too overpowering or not high-powered enough! I asked
where that left me and he grinned and said, 'Somewhere in
the middle, about right I think!' Having looked around what I
thought was of all the farms, later I realised I had only seen a
part of them, as there were some problem areas which subsequently came to light. I asked where it was anticipated I would
live? I thought at least I should have some idea. Manor Farm
at Molescroft was a rather unusual old farmhouse with nine-
teen rooms.

Having had a most interesting but trying sort of day, my
head was spinning with what I had seen, some good, some
mediocre and some downright bloody awful. It was obvious
just from looking around that over the years, advantage had
been taken by some of the former caretakers of the business
and all was not as it should have been. I later found out that
there had been quite a bit of fiddling going on. I was asked to
wait outside for ten minutes after the interview, whilst John
had a word with the owner. I tried to collect my thoughts and
had decided that it was beyond a challenge. Eventually, John
emerged and said that the owner wanted me to take the job
and I could name my price. He was a very persuasive man was
John and thirty minutes later I found myself accepting what
turned out to be probably the best move I ever made in my life
– eventually!

I popped up every weekend from Billingborough, to look
around the farms and to see what was going on, and to develop a feel for the place until it was time to move. I remember
one weekend finding a gang of men leading straw bales - one
man sitting on a tractor, four men forking the small bales with
two more men on a trailer and they were all on overtime. The

machinery was old and very dilapidated, the tractors as such were in a bad state of repair; I found one had not had an oil change for a couple of years and I found a drill under a hedge bottom, with its back broken. Rusty implements were laying everywhere, and the potato crops looked awful, they subsequently yielded six tonnes per acre. Wet holes existed all over the place, as three of the four farms were at or below river level and there had been a problem with the drainage. Some of the land was called Carr land, which meant it was a bit peaty, a bit wet and a bit fluffy, very difficult to consolidate.

Bog oak is a feature of this land and we spent many an hour digging out large lengths of the stuff and we finished up with quite a big heap of it and take it from me, it is very hard to saw, and it used to play hell with drainage machines. I have some in my garden, which is quite effective and by carbon dating is deemed to be 7000 years old. One thing Carr land is good at growing is root crops and also grass.

I moved in on the 2 September 1969. An Aga cooker had been installed and most of the work completed on the house, although I never did get central heating. There was only one telephone, so I ran some cabling myself all around the place so at least I wouldn't have a root march every time it rang and ring it did. News travels fast and every representative from every company wanted to call. I told them all the same that I would be happy to see them, either before seven in the morning or after six in the evening. That sorted one or two out! The farm had a contract to supply pigs to the FMC, [1] but none had gone there, so this had to be resolved. The Jersey cows, not great yielders at the best of times, were not milking at all well and had had a succession of herd managers, all with their own ideas. They were also proving difficult to get in calf. The first

1. Fatstock Marketing Corporation.

morning, the recently appointed herd manager asked me if he could open up the cake bag. [2] I asked him if he thought that would do the job or was there a more fundamental problem? There was a more fundamental problem, in fact several. There was a relief chap on the pigs who was not in the least bit interested in the 120 pedigree large White sows, and there was resentment from some of the arable staff, who had had a cosy relationship with the foreman who was leaving and had been able to pick and choose their jobs. Harvest had not finished. We had two drying set ups, one a continuous flow and on floor storage, the other an in-bin affair. Two old combines were incapable of keeping both going, yet neither of the driers could cope with both combines. That meant a lot of ducking and diving on a daily basis. The first week I went home at ten in the evening with a splitting headache, wondering what on earth I had done. The next week it was nine, still with a headache, then eight, and after that the headache disappeared. If my memory serves me correctly, there were fifty-two different fields on the farm, some obviously not very big which caused problems, fortunately several were grass fields for the cows, and handy to the dairy. I believe we had every kind of soil you could think of, which meant careful planning of the cropping, and I well recall Birds Eye for whom we grew vining peas, would not entertain any field under ten acres in size. Some fields were less than that, and had no chance of being joined to the next one in many cases because of ditches.

Each month I had a visit from Lugg and Gould who would physically grill me as to progress and if not why not, that sort of thing. We did a ten year forward plan, including a substantial capital investment programme, which would see some

2. Feed concentrates came in a bag and the feed was referred to as cake, as originally years ago, linseed and cotton seed came in slabs known as cake.

new tractors trailers and machinery, plus a new cubicle house for the cows, a new piggery, some updating for the two farms where we had the eighteen month beef enterprises, a new chitting store, work on the two potato stores and drainage. In those days there were excellent grants available of which we took full advantage, but it meant an awful lot of paperwork, but the good thing was that the Ministry of Agriculture office was in Beverley and once I had found out who I needed to talk to I found them exceedingly helpful.

We were members of Blue Group, one of the several pea vining consortiums set up to supply Birds Eye. During the four years I was there, we never made any money out of vining peas. My first year was so dry that we did not have a drop of rain from sowing date to harvesting, consequently the crop was not good. The next year we had foot rot in the peas and they were rejected. The year after that it rained all the time and the fields were left in a mess and half the peas run over whilst in the fourth year, I had the best crop of peas you could wish for but they were by-passed and had to be cut for seed. There were no such things as self-propelled viners then, and each member of the group had to supply at least one tractor and sometimes two men. A separate tractor mounted pea cutter went in front of the viners, leaving the peas in a neat row for the viner to pick up. The supplying of labour caused problems as there was no farm transport available at that time for the men to use and not all of them had their own cars. On top of that the viners could finish up miles away from where they started so the vehicles would never be in the right place anyway. So I had a dilemma. I either let them use my farm transport and use my own car for the farm, or I could take them and fetch them back again. One year I sent a new chap to the viners and as he was towing one along, he managed to get one of the wheels off the road into some soft ground and it simply turned over onto its side. It is not a pretty sight seeing such an enormous machine, belly up! That of course caused more problems as one viner out of action cut down capacity enormously. I think in truth it needed a bigger, heavier tractor, which I did not have. I was not a popular man.

Taking labour away at that time of year just prior to and into harvest, made life difficult on the farms also as most of the men had families and wanted to have their holidays with the children, so juggling the two was not easy. At harvest time I had the benefit of having the boss's chauffeur as a combine driver. He always came at the beginning of harvest and stayed until we had finished. He was a very good mechanic and serviced the combines daily whilst the other driver was about other jobs on the farm. He also came each year at the end of September to put anti-freeze into every tractor and vehicle on the farm. The boss very wisely went away at harvest time on his yacht. I think that was why I was allowed to have Thorpe for the combine. The boss had a long wheel base Land Rover Safari, probably the numbest vehicle I have ever driven. He always had a Jaguar and one of the first of the XJ6 models, as well as his superb Bentley Continental. I think the Land Rover and the Jaguar were run by the farm and the Bentley by the Fishing Company.

One year he came to see me just before he went on holiday to tell me that Thorpe was available and that I had to keep him no matter what, even if a request from the headquarters on the fish docks came through, absolutely nothing was to take Thorpe away. We were about two-thirds of the way through this particular harvest when the boss, who had returned early from holiday, came into the field with his Land Rover. He made his way towards me and asked that I send Thorpe to him immediately. Apparently, he had had a puncture in the Bentley on the way home and wanted to send Thorpe out to put four new tyres on immediately. I jokingly reminded him that nothing was to take Thorpe away, to which he replied, 'Walton, this is different!'

The Hull Scarborough railway line ran through the middle of the farm and quite frankly it was a damned nuisance. Opening and shutting the gates was a time-consuming bore, particularly if we were leading corn across, as we were obliged to close them every time. The cows grazed across the other side of the line in the summer and we had to ring the station to let them know when we were going to cross, and they would then say if we could. We had to ring them back again when the cows had made their way across. One day the cowman forgot and a train was kept in the station for quite a while. After that the staff at the railway were not so helpful. One Saturday night, a taxi collected one of the men from Carr Farm and took a short cut across the railway so as to cut off three miles of the journey. Officially the driver should not have done this for it was for farm use only. Not being used to the crossing, the driver drove his taxi off it and got one of the wheels in front of a track and the rear wheels behind the adjacent line. He could not move an inch. He quickly bundled the passengers out and ran down the line but to no avail, a train was coming and it smashed into the taxi, carrying it a hundred yards down the track. It was as though it had been put in a car crusher. The front bogey of the train had been pushed back about five or six yards, and it slewed across the track, preventing the trains coming down the opposite line.

This happened about eight at night and the police rang for me to go down where they tore a strip off me, as if it was my fault. Next morning the phone rang at ten past six, it was the boss. He had heard the news on the local radio and wondered if it was our crossing? He was not best pleased when I confirmed that it was, I received a lecture about safety on the railway, which I could well have done without. I had already made it clear to the staff that the crossing was for farm use only, but you cannot be responsible for everybody all the time.

John, whom I mentioned in a previous chapter, the one with the ancient cycle, had a nasty experience once at Carr Farm. At that time there was no one actually living there, so each night at bedtime, I used to drive down to the farm to make sure that the bulling heifers we had there were alright, and to make sure that gates and things were closed. One night I found a light on in one of the sheds. I switched it off but found it on again the next night. This time I found a half bottle of milk, which by the next night had been emptied. I realised then that someone must be sleeping in the buildings, but try as I might I couldn't catch them. It was during the winter and John went every morning to give the heifers their feed and straw up the yard. He used to use the crossing on his cycle, once he had completed his task. One particular morning he had not returned by the normal time and as I was going that way I thought I would just check to make sure all was fine. I found John looking like a ghost, sitting on a bale of straw. I asked him what the problem was and he just pointed to the line. The vagabond or tramp or whoever he was had lain down by the side of the track and an oncoming train had chopped his head off.

It was not a pretty sight and it knocked John for six and I told him to have a few days off to recover. I immediately phoned the police who arrived in force. I suppose they are used to incidents like that and are perhaps a bit callous in such situations. They picked the head up by the hair, looked at it, asked if anyone recognised it then put it in a plastic bag. They had brought a plastic coffin with them to take the body away. John was off work again later when he had to give evidence at the inquest.

John usually was very dry and droll. I remember one Sunday morning going down to the farm just to have a look around and make sure that all was well with the heifers when I found John strawing up. I asked him if everything was in order and he pointed to a heifer that was obviously dead and said, 'I don't think that one is very well'. I still don't know whether he was having me on or not.

Having a large mixed farm with pigs, dairy and beef, could lead to problems with staff. Naturally, we wanted the first cut silage for the cows, and for 250 cows and followers we needed quite a bit. We also had two other self-feed silage yards, one at Manor Farm and the other at Storkhill Farm. The chap who reared our calves and was officially the beast man had a real knack at rearing and loved his animals. I remember once we had been dehorning some calves and a couple of them were bleeding quite badly. He disappeared into another shed and came back with a handful of cobwebs, which he proceeded to stick onto the bleeding horns. The blood dried up almost immediately, I have never forgotten that. He used to get a bit uptight about the silage, thinking that he was the poor relation, always having what he considered second best as the infernal Jerseys had to have first quality. Bert was another character. One of his eyes would revolve when he looked at you and particularly if he was getting upset. He had the most wonderful command of Yorkshire dialect – well actually he got things a bit muddled up. His wife used to have trouble with her back. I asked him one day how she was and he replied that she had one of those 'kleptomatic' backs, whatever they were. Each week he filled in his time sheet with the hours he had worked on his various jobs, as all labour was apportioned to each sector wherever possible. Bert spent most of his time in the winter at least, with the cattle, and he always put down on the sheet the time spent amongst cattle as 'bollocks' instead of bullocks! As the wages and the financial records were done on the docks at headquarters, I think Bert's time sheets used to amuse the young girls in the office. I think perhaps his best one was when his wife had to go into hospital for a hysterectomy. He came to the door one day all excitable to tell me that the missus had to have one of 'them there hysterical rectomies'!

Sam on East Yorkshire coast, 1958.

7 | Taking a Farm

The first year passed so quickly, I hardly seemed to have time to breathe. Having arrived halfway through the financial year I was very conscious that the results for that year were not going to be good. As I previously stated, the potatoes only yielded six tonnes to the acre and the cost of getting them up equalled the income. Harvest had not been brilliant, so I had to ensure the best possible sales and really there was little else I could do to influence the outcome. The pigs were in a mess, production having slipped quite badly, so all I could do was to sell the ones we had for the best possible price. I remember the boss nearly had a duck fit when I bought a Landrace boar from Peter Brier of Mossbrook. I suppose the days of the pedigree herds was beginning to diminish, so I thought that we would have a bit of hybrid vigour into the Large Whites, or at least some of them. I would love to have used a different bull on the Jerseys to get some value into the calves, but that area was strictly taboo.

I did, however, manage to persuade the boss to try a couple of inseminations of Charolais on some of the older pedigree cows. In actual fact, they were good and we reared them on the beef unit. Normally the male calves, if not good enough for breeding, used to go to the kennels for the hounds. Showing the Jerseys was part of the job but it never appealed to me in any way. Fortunately, the herdsmen were all enthusiastic and we did have many successes, but I never reconciled that with extra pedigree sales. I am not a cow man. I had a fair idea what made Friesians tick but I had no notion what made Jerseys. I had a blood test done on the whole herd to see if any were deficient in minerals. Cystic ovaries were a common feature and although we could sell all the milk we could get, I never really did enthuse about them. We used to bottle milk for a local dairyman, by a hand operated machine, which would have looked well in the museum, along with John's bike! It used to break down frequently and caused me no end of bother. Spare parts were only available from a firm in London, which meant many a night I had to meet the late train in Hull as parts were sent by Red Star.

It is essential, not only with your own farming, to set out your objectives, but it is probably even more important to know what your employer's aims are. I knew that as far as the boss and his wife were concerned the Jerseys were their special interest, the breeding and the showing, and they had to be made as viable as possible. That was not always easy and was an area in which I failed miserably. The rest of the farm staff thought there was favouritism of the dairy and its staff, and if money was spent there and not in their own sections, they would get quite upset.

We managed to get most of the improvements done to the farms, and by the time I left four years later, the enormous deficit of the first year had been turned into a bigger surplus.

Moving from the management of 1000 acres to what was then 107 acres to start farming on my own account was as big a step as when I went to the 1000 acres. I remember going to see the bank manager, whom I had never met and whose name I did not even know. I asked one of the women in the bank what his name was and if he had ten minutes to spare. She told me his name was Alan Hamilton and that he could fit me in for ten minutes. I used to think that bank managers, sitting behind their enormous desks were very intimidating. I recall what the late Frank Arden [1] once said, that when you borrow your first £10,000 you get a coffee, when it is £100,000 the manager gets

1 Frank Arden, in his day, was the biggest farmer in the United Kingdom.

the sherry bottle out. Nowadays, the manager comes to me for coffee, so I am not sure what that means, perhaps the bank can no longer afford the coffee or the sherry!

However, on that day I did not feel the least bit intimidated, I was very confident and I knew he would sanction a loan. After I sat down (no coffee) and we had exchanged pleasantries or at least I thought they were, he asked how he could help? I said, 'I have just taken a farm'. His jaw dropped as he looked at the very small thin piece of paper with my life history on so far as the bank was concerned and he sort of spluttered, 'With what?' I didn't bat an eyelid, I simply said, 'With some of your money I hope'. He peered over his specs and said, 'I have never had an approach like that before, how much do you want?' I replied, 'Only £5,000'. 'You can have £1,500', he said, to which I replied, 'Done', got up, shook hands and walked out after fixing the rate at 2.5% above base rate. So with that and what little I already had, is how I started farming.

I daresay it could not be done today. At that time inflation was really beginning to take off, so I suppose apart from an initial hiccup that worked in my favour. I bought six gilts in pig from the farms I was managing, and made sure that I paid the proper price which then was £45 each. I managed to find an old Fordson Dexta tractor which had just been re-bored and for that I paid the princely sum of £300. It had a muck loader attached but was a nightmare to steer without power steering. I attended the farm sale when the previous tenant left, bought an old Fergy trailer, a vice, a roller grinder in the meal house, a set of seed harrows, and a couple of well-grown calves, plus a brush and shovel, and a wheelbarrow along with an old fuel tank.

It is quite an eerie feeling to walk around an empty farmstead. It is the one and only time I have ever done that. There were no modern buildings whatsoever on the farm, the loose boxes were still half full of manure, and in the cattle yard next to the house a tap reigned supreme above the tank. The first thing I did was to put a ball cock into the tank. Alix, who had worked on the farm for thirty-five years, and who wanted to retire came to see me, his son was subsequently to work for me for twenty-two years, and I proudly showed him the new ball valve arrangement. He just nodded and said, 'All things are relative, a tap was better than a pump handle!'

The spring of 1973 was very early, dry and bright. The farm had been sown to a third of the arable acreage with what we know in Yorkshire as away going crop. When a tenant leaves, he is permitted to sow a third of his eligible arable into wheat or whatever. He sows it and then does nothing with it. The incoming tenant can either leave it, or 'farm it' properly. The crop is estimated by two valuers, one for the incomer and another for the outgoer, about a week before harvest. In other words, they estimate the yield. You then pay the outgoer the following spring. So you are in a cleft stick. The outgoer may have put a bit of fertiliser on, maybe not. He may have used a weed spray, again, maybe not. So the more you, as the ingoer does to the crop, the more money you put into the outgoer's pocket.

This is where I came unstuck. I had never really sold wheat at much above £34 a tonne previously and when I was offered £44 a tonne, straight off the combine, for all of the away going crop, I jumped at it. That sounds fine, but by the time the price of the away going crop was settled which was in the January of the next year, the price had risen to nearly £60 a tonne and I had to pay that to the outgoer. On top of that, the yield was nowhere as good as had been estimated, but I still had to pay on the estimated yield, which was well over half a tonne per acre more. I think the idea originally was to protect the landlord, in case of rent default by the tenant. Perhaps it is time now for this archaic system to be done away with once and for all. The following year wheat was £65 a tonne and then into the seventies. As I write this over thirty years later, wheat is again back to that price and lower.

The farm was due to be taken over on the 6 April, but as I had permission to enter early, the whole lot was sown up by the 5 February. There had been lots of five acre blocks in most of the fields. It gave me huge satisfaction to see the contractor plough through the whole lot of them to make reasonable sized acreages. I had approached a contractor I knew, who had a large operation. I told him the position that I was not particularly flush, but I would use him for as long as it mutually suited us both. He said I could have credit till harvest time if I needed it. I found I didn't need to do that and sent him a cheque by return. He came down the next day and thanked me, and told me that in all his years he had never ever had a cheque by return and asked what else would I like doing? We had a long working relationship together until the firm was sold up. He always came when I needed him and I always paid him. I had by this time negotiated a bigger loan, up to my £5,000. I had bought 23 bullocks in readiness for turning out onto the permanent grass and had also bought some ewes in lamb and had started to rear calves. All this was going on whilst I still had my job on the 1,000 acres, as well as altering buildings as fast as I could go. I was just a bit busy.

Neighbours, particularly farming neighbours are great. I saw one of them in the local market one day when I was having lunch. He said, 'You have 23 grand bullocks in that yard'. I asked him how he knew and he replied, 'Oh, I have counted them!' 'Thank you', was my reply. 'Perhaps you would like to count them every day and keep an eye on them for me?'

I did not move into the farm house until that July. I had also bought at the sale, to use as a second vehicle, the ten year-old Hillman car for £40, which in all that time had only covered 30,000 miles. I used it for taking churns of hot water each day to feed the calves. It was an absolute rot box, so I was pleased to sell it on for £45.

I remember the first harvest. We had all small bales and would stack them in the fields where each crop had been grown. This saved time at harvest and at that time I only had one flat trailer. By the second harvest I had actually bought an elevator for these damned bales. However, in the first harvest, feeling strong, I rather foolishly forked the bales. I certainly could not and would not want to these days. I decided I could not afford to buy polythene sheets to put over the bale stacks, so adopted an idea I had seen in operation in Scotland, which was to leave the top two rows of bales with wind tunnels between them, allowing the wind to blow through the stack. It was reasonably successful, although inevitably there was some waste. The next day I noticed one of my neighbours had done the same thing, followed later by another neighbour. I dropped across both of them one day having a chat (there was always time to have a chat, whatever happened to that?) and I remarked that I was pleased to see that I had obviously chosen the right method of protecting straw, and how long had they both done that? I was staggered at their reply: 'We watched you do it and as you are a bit of a whizz kid we thought it must be the thing to do, so we copied you!'

I had been quite pleased with the production of the eighteen-month beef on the farms at Molescroft. We used to graze the cattle on a third of the acreage allotted to them, take silage off two thirds, then let the cattle graze the aftermath, shut up the first third for silage, and then finally allow the cattle

to have all the area. I tried a similar stunt here, although not
to make silage, it would have to be hay. Cattle do not put on
weight as quickly with worn out permanent pasture, and try
as I might with two young beasts to the acre they just were not
performing, despite a fertiliser regime. I was looking at them
one day when the father of one of my neighbours strolled past.
He came and leaned on the gate also and asked how I thought
they were doing. I didn't swear, as he was a very religious man,
but I felt like it! He nodded and said, 'I could have told you
they wouldn't do, you need stronger cattle there and fewer of
them!' I looked at him and said, 'Yes, but you *didn't* tell me',
and he just smiled a very knowing smile.

I tried to build up livestock enterprises, as I had by then
got up to 20 sows by selling weaners. I soon found out that
rearing calves was a toil of a pleasure, for when you sold them
at twelve weeks of age, it cost you the same as they made to replace them because of inflation. I sold all the ewes with lambs
at foot as I had nowhere to graze them in the summer. For a
number of years I bought broken-mouthed old ewes in the autumn, borrowed a couple of Suffolk tups from a local breeder,
for which he only wanted a bottle of Scotch, sold them again
with lambs at foot and in all the time I did that, they never
failed to double their purchase price. The first year I had a bit
of twin lamb disease in some of them and had the vet out a
couple of times. One day, one of the partners who hadn't visited before arrived at the farm. I had seen him, knew of him,
but had never met him. As we walked up the field to the ewes
he turned to me and said, 'Don't worry, when I have treated
this ewe, she will get up and run away'. She did - then dropped
down dead after fifty yards! John looked at me and said, 'I did
say it would get up and run!' We both roared with laughter
and that was the start of a very firm friendship, which existed

until his sad death in June 2000, only five years after his early retirement. Shortly after that episode, John bought a house in our village, where he continued to live with his charming wife Margaret. I remember taking a tractor and trailer to fetch his garden shed and other odds and sods when he moved in. He proved invaluable over the years and very convenient too, living in the village. He was always very popular with his clients and a great hit in the village. He didn't specialise in any one particular thing, but had a sound common sense approach to all sectors. Their practice had a wide spread of interests including the local greyhound racing which they supervised, lecturing at Bishop Burton College, and one vet was full time doing meat inspection.

We have had lots of laughs together. One New Year's Eve, John was at the farm and had switched his phone through. As it approached midnight a call came in from someone in Hull who had a problem with a dog. He did not recognise the person, asked them if he was a client to which the man replied, 'No, but I didn't like to disturb my normal vet'. John agreed to see the dog if the man could bring it through to the surgery in Beverley. I went along with him and this man complete with cigarette-smoking wife and half-a-dozen sniffling children turned up with their mongrel. As they approached us John said something like, 'I bet he hasn't much money poor sod, I won't be able to charge him much'. I don't remember what the problem was, but he fixed up the dog and the man asked how much it cost. John replied, '£7.50 please'. The man pulled out the biggest wad of tenners I have ever seen and said, 'I thought it would have been fifty quid!' You can imagine what John said on the way home. Another time I went with him late at night to visit one of his clients, who although very well-off did not like spending money. He had a gilt that was not getting on with farrowing very well and he wanted some help having failed himself to relieve her. John examined her and decided a hysterectomy would be the answer. He duly phoned his fellow vet who was on duty requesting he bring all the necessary gear to perform the operation. The client was at least 25 miles from the surgery and the other vet lived even further away. Eventually by two in the morning everything was ready, the operation was carried out and as the owner stood there ready to count the large litter, the gilt produced a single pig. You should have seen his face! It must surely have been one of the most expensive pigs ever!

I suppose if John had a favourite animal it was probably horses. My wife has always bred horses, and horses to my mind always seem to need the vet for something. When asked after pregnancy testing a mare, which he did for lots of people, whether the foal would be a colt or a filly, he would always tell the farmer one thing but write the opposite in his book. He had two chances of being right, and if he was right, he would tell the farmer, 'I told you so', and if he was wrong he would look in his book and show the farmer that he had written down exactly what the farmer had got. It worked every time.

John was very good with people as well as animals. He only ever wanted to look after animals; he hated all the paper work associated with the business, the rules, the regulations, the red tape. The day he actually became the senior partner (for like most vet groups who work their way up the ladder, and as partners retire, young assistants are given the chance to mortgage themselves up to the hilt to buy into the practice), John went upstairs to wade through all the papers ready for him on the desk. No sooner had he sat down than the five women from reception and the nursing side all trooped up and stood in front of his desk. Whilst he continued looking through his papers, one of the assembled group said they had come to seek a rise, so he simply said, 'Yes, fine, you can have one, but when you get downstairs decide which one of you is leaving'. He never heard any more on the subject. He did have too an enormous sense of fun and humour and told the story of the door bell ringing one morning at two-thirty, and when he went to answer, it was a lady in her nightdress clutching a cat, who said, 'Would you like to examine my pussy?'

At one time he always ran Ford cars. He changed them every year and one year the new model had all the hand controls on the opposite side from that to which he had been accustomed. He was called out early one morning and was stopped by the local constabulary. The officer approached the car, asked him the usual questions as to why was he out at that time of morning, had he been drinking, and would he please operate the car lights? As John went to do that a jet of water was sent into the officer's eyes; he had not got used to the different controls. That was typical of John, as grand a chap as you could possibly meet. That was confirmed to me at his funeral when the large St Mary's Church in Beverley was crammed to capacity. I, like many more, miss him a lot.

Commercial ACI sows and piglets from ACMC

Good example of Saddleback sow

Saddleback with litter

8 | Adopting Children

After the first year at Village Farm, I had developed a mixed bag of enterprises and it was when he left school that Nick, son of the chap who used to work on the farm came to work for me. At first, I had a job to get him near machinery and tractors. It didn't take long for him to develop though, he went to Bishop Burton College on various courses and by the time he moved on, he had been ploughing, drilling, spraying, and top dressing to a very high standard and was a very useful chap to have. He also developed a feel for livestock and I had no hesitation in leaving him on his own for days on end, as my work with *Pig World* grew and grew, encouraging him to make decisions.

I had married again two years after going to the farms at Beverley. My wife is the daughter of a very successful arable farming family in Derbyshire and had worked at home ever since leaving school. We met at a Young Farmers Ambassadors' reunion in Buxton. Ellen had visited America on the exchange scheme and of course I had been to Rhodesia. She is a natural stock person and has had horses since she was three years old, so she was very useful to have around the place. She is probably the finest judge of a horse in the country, but I have little interest in them and they have often proved a bone of contention between us. They seem to eat all the best grass, ruin all the fences and forever need either the vet or the blacksmith. They are a worry at foaling needing carting to a stud, insurance costs a fortune, they bite at one end, kick at the other and I think they are damned uncomfortable in between!

The day we actually took this farm and before I bought any of the stuff at the sale, I had a Volvo 144, a box of spanners and nothing else, not even a brush and shovel. Ellen had a Rice horse trailer, and the combination of car and trailer did a lot

of work. It flitted us from one farm to the other and I took all
sorts of livestock in it. Eventually, we swapped that for a lorry
and I had a farm lorry on the books, varying from the old T. K.
Bedfords, to a Renault and finally a Mercedes, until 1994. The
latter I had for nine years and it never cost a penny other than
servicing, one exhaust, and a set of tyres.

Although I had grandfather rights for an operators' licence
I decided I should really sit the exam to gain a CPC, which is
a Certificate of Personal Competence, to actually be in charge
of a haulage business. That was an interesting experience. Although I no longer have a lorry I still have the certificate. We
were able over the years to do a bit of haulage, things like delivering seed corn and of course livestock. Sometimes I went,
sometimes Nick would go, and then the better half would be
raked in also. I doubt if there is any money to be made in haulage these days, the price of fuel is horrendous. For a number of
years we delivered our own pigs, and I met all sorts of interesting people and saw some very different farms. I think there is
no doubt that to obtain the best return from pigs, you need to
breed and finish. As I was always building up and improving
the buildings and buying specialised pig buildings, I always
seemed to need the money and the room, so we didn't finish
pigs in any quantity until a couple of years before I sold out of
pigs. At one time we got up to 220 sows producing weaners;
it was too many which put pressure on the unit. We cut back
again to around 140 and tried to finish them by altering yet
more buildings. Being in the middle of a village and the farm
yard being on a slope could have proved difficult. Fortunately,
we have good neighbours, at least most of them. Occasionally
we would get an interloper who would complain about something or other, and a couple of times we had a bit of a flood
when some pretty unsavoury looking liquid ran down into the

street and then into the beck which runs through the village. Enough said!

Moving into the house here was an interesting experience. The previous couple had lived here a good number of years and unfortunately the tenant had died. Electricity had been put in, but only the bare minimum, inasmuch as there was a two-pin plug at the top of the stairs which had to serve two of the bedrooms. There was a single light in each room and only one plug in the kitchen and in each of the other rooms. I think our local electrician thought I was magic, as I had a new ring mains put in upstairs and another one downstairs, plus as many electric points as you could fit in. The same had applied in the farm buildings, one lamp hanging above a dividing wall between two loose boxes served both boxes, or should I say didn't really serve any useful purpose at all.

I noticed that there were eight cracked window panes in the house, of which the one in the kitchen windows had an eighth of an inch gap in it, through which a howling gale was blowing. I commented to the lady who was vacating the house that it seemed a pity that on the point of leaving they should have suffered so many broken windows, and how had it happened? She replied she did not know as they were like that when they had moved in thirty-six years previously!

The first thing I did was to install an oil-fired Aga which cost £265 fitted (it now costs more than that to fill the 1,000 litres tank) and has never had anything wrong with it in years, apart from routine servicing items, all other parts are original. I would think today that we would be looking at closer to £5,000 for the same thing. We had two old pantries that had tiled floors laid straight onto the soil and distempered walls. They were quickly altered into one room, which was subsequently knocked through into one of the front rooms, to make a large

The infamous Aga.

lounge dining room area. Having been there for twelve years
we decided to enlarge the house and to make it more accessible. The kitchen was extended and a rear entrance built on,
which joined us up to a range of old loose boxes, part of which
is now my office, the remainder a large utility room with a
couple of double sinks. Both areas have proved invaluable. We
did various other alterations. I did away with the pigs being
near the house, knocked down an old range of buildings and
made the cattle yard next to the house into a garden, which I
am pleased to say has matured into an interesting and attrac-

tive area, complete with pond. I am not and never have been much of a gardener but I do enjoy seeing a nice garden. I find mowing the lawns rather therapeutic.

In 1974 our adopted daughter Romney, arrived at the age of six weeks and on my birthday. I can't think of a nicer birthday present. She was a blue-eyed blonde and has been a delight the whole of her life. It was fascinating watching her grow and develop. She has never had any fear of animals and spent ages amongst the pigs. In 1977, she was joined by our adopted son, Victor, who at thirteen days old, arrived on my wife's birthday. Neither of them ever gave us a disturbed night and they have never been any problem. I think they enjoyed life on the farm, they both rode ponies from a very early age, Romney became an excellent rider, competing in the local pony club events the length and breadth of the land. She used to terrify me as she seemed absolutely fearless. Victor was more restrained. I don't think in all honesty that it appealed to him too much. One thing that was drilled into them both was that when they had ridden, the ponies had to be groomed, fed and watered, their stables mucked out and their tack cleaned, before they fed themselves. I believe that to be good discipline, having seen a lot of spoiled young brats at various times who would throw a paddy rather than work at their responsibilities. Very often in these situations I believe it is the parents who are keener than the children, and would get very wound up if their offspring did not win. The pony days have now long gone but there is a board in my office covered in rosettes.

We are none of us trained in the bringing up of children; I suppose we fly by the seat of our pants. It was decided that we would try to give them both a good education, which is probably the best thing any parent can do. At least they have something to work on. I would not like to start to do that again today, it is financially prohibitive. Ellen said she would go out to work, which she did, and now the children are grown up and away she is still working, as a senior care officer with people who have learning difficulties. I can't decide whether she likes the job, or the money, or the fact it gets her away from me!

I don't know whether or not adopting children is easier or more difficult than having your own. I suppose the way we did it at least we got what we wanted and we knew when they were arriving. Living on a farm provides you a wonderful opportunity of telling the children about adoption. We told them all the time and when I felt Romney was old enough to understand, I took her into a farrowing house one day and explained that one sow had too many pigs, while another didn't have enough, so we swapped a couple over, explaining at the same

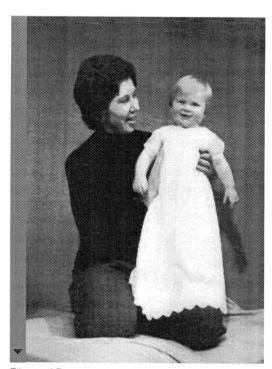

Ellen and Romney.

Rom and Vic on their first pony, Noddy.

time that that was how adoption worked. It must have made an impression on her because the next day she had been back in again and moved the whole lot onto one sow, she thought a big family would be better!

Funny what children do and how they think. One day I had been working in a farrowing house and Romney had quietly shut the door and fastened it, leaving me a virtual prisoner in the shed. I had to physically kick the door down to get out and when I asked her why she had done it, she replied that she wanted to make sure that I was looking after the adopted family!

We are lucky in the village inasmuch as we have a superb village school. Both went there until the age of eight. Romney then went to Hull High School for Girls at Tranby Croft in Hull, did very well, obtaining ten O levels. She decided she would like to go to Pocklington School for the Sixth Form, which is where Victor was being educated. It certainly made transport a lot easier, and she managed to pass her four A levels quite comfortably. Victor is a much more reserved sort of lad and although he gained five O levels, he has always had to work at whatever he did. He did much better in his A levels than anticipated which gave him a big boost. He excelled at French and speaks it like a native and for many years went to France each summer to stay with his pen pal. I think he has wander-lust or the travel bug, I can't decide which. By the time he was sixteen, he had been to America three times, twice on his own. He has been all over Europe, Greece and Turkey. He really wanted to work in airport or airline management. Romney never wanted anything other than to be a teacher. She is brilliant with children. She went to Leeds University for four years, gained an honours degree and immediately took off to work in Kuwait, teaching English at the Anglo–Arab Academy. Everybody missed her dreadfully.

Victor wanted to do tourism and French and went to Bolton to study. Having applied to all the airlines, he was told the same thing - apply again once he had some experience. Whilst he was still studying, he got himself a part time job with a large multiple clothing retailer which he loved. When he left college he worked there full time for a while but on a part time arrangement, if that makes sense. I think we all felt this was an unsatisfactory arrangement but the big companies try this on as it saves sick pay and holidays. They kept promising him a full time contract and a year's trainee management course but it never seemed to materialise.

He was living in Leeds by this time, having rented a house with a pal of his. One day he saw an advertisement for a job at the Halifax on 24-hour telephone banking, applied and got the job. He immediately told the store of his job offer and they tried everything to get him to stay, saying they were about to give him this contract. The outcome was that he agreed to work there in the evenings or on some of his days off, so in a way he had the best of both worlds.

I made sure that Romney and Victor had the opportunity to drive on the farm as soon as they were allowed. They got quite good at handling tractors and I bought an old banger in which they both raced around the paddocks until it met its end. As soon as they were seventeen, I bought each of them a car and some driving lessons. I am proud that they are both excellent drivers, very natural the pair of them as they have a feel for the vehicle. In her first year of driving, Romney did 18,000 miles! Victor beat that by doing 20,000. I tried to instil in them that vehicles were to be looked after properly, checked at least once a week and serviced when due. I also told them that if they missed one service, or had one drink and then drove, that the respective car would be sold. It worked wonders. Victor and I had a long chat about farming. He always helped when asked, but is not a born farmer and I wouldn't wish it on anyone these days, unless it was a larger farm, bought and paid for. I asked if he would like to come home and farm and that we would start another enterprise to justify his existence. He said, 'No, I don't think so Dad, there is no money in it'. I asked him what made him say that and he grinned and replied, 'You are always telling me that', to which I responded, 'At least you take note of some of the things I say'. He then added that shovelling shit would not look very good on his CV!

Without doubt the most difficult thing to do on a small farm is to develop enterprises that bring in the cash. I felt it was sensible to grow seed corn as the farm was wild oat free and clean otherwise. There was then a £15 per tonne premium which all helped. I had installed some bins with air ducts in the bottom and a series of fans. This enabled me to keep varieties separate and to dry the corn, provided it was not too wet. If it was wet it meant emptying the bins out and re-loading them again, to make sure the corn was well turned and mixed. I sometimes found solid patches in the bins, as the air always takes the line of least resistance. It was hard work shovelling the bins out, so eventually I sold them and built an on-floor corn store capable of holding 600 tonnes. The shed where the bins had been was then converted into dry sow yards and later into finishing yards.

Ten years after taking the farm, the landlord put another 70 acres on to it. I had rented a field from a neighbour to grow vegetables and had also rented two fields from another neighbour, some 22 acres on which to graze cattle. My late father-in-law allowed me to rent his riverside meadows for grazing, some 30 acres and in 1977 I had managed to rent from the Ministry of Defence another 22 acres on the aerodrome at Leconfield, which I had for twenty-four years, before they took it back in order to plant trees. So at one time I had five different landlords.

I decided to increase output by growing vegetables, and for many years I grew calabrese, double cropping about seven acres. We also had a go at cauliflowers for freezing, along with sprouts. For several years I would drive to Leeds market after tea, with calabrese and caulis in their season, sometimes three times a week. I had bought a one tonne capacity two-wheeled trailer to tow behind a car or a pick-up, and I had that for sixteen years without so much as a puncture. It cost me £350 to buy and I sold it for £150 after all that time. The reason I gave up on vegetables was that I was not prepared to spend the money necessary for a packing plant with all the paraphalialia. Cling film wrapping was coming in, the fresh market price didn't increase at all over the period, but the cost of labour and packaging had rocketed. Nevertheless, I have no regrets about having grown this produce as it gave me an insight to a totally different world. On the large field scale, whilst producing cauliflowers for one outlet, I got dropped in for £10,000. That is a lot of money today, but it was a hell of a lot more then!

The whole place buzzed for a while and I had also set up a bull beef enterprise in one of the yards, which would take 60 head. Grass seed also featured for three years, but I had a legacy of Italian ryegrass that for years after I called the new arable weed. I took full advantage of the capital grants available and bought seven Lindrick containerised piggeries, and when I got rid of the bulls, which I believe each lost £35 a head on the last batch, I then altered the yards into extra farrowing.

Never in my wildest calculations did I envisage that a small farm could gobble up so much capital. I was in full flow for many years, a bit of a hell-fire jack I suppose, but I was so enjoying what I was doing.

It does seem strange that every time you take on some land, it needs some work doing to it. The land on the airfield, which is now the Army Driving School, had been spring barley and wild oats for twenty-two years. I wanted it for growing vegetables. Having ploughed the land, I worked Avadex into the soil, but despite that, there was still a massive crop of wild oats that appeared. We then cultivated the land again to kill them, and we did that three times with three different germinations before we drilled it with calabrese and planted cauliflowers; we then steerage hoed the crops and still managed to pull seven trailer loads of wild oats out of the growing crop. I had never seen anything like it in my life. The contractor retired and sold up in 1984, so I decided that we would do all the work ourselves, with the exception of the combining. I have never owned a combine, never had any desire to own one, I am sure that many times my acreage is required to even justify one. I had had various tractors on the farm and we had been doing things like rolling, some power harrowing and spraying for a while, leaving the contractor to do the ploughing, sowing, combining and baling. I have never owned a baler either and would not want to.

So, in a rush of blood to the head one day, I went out and bought another Fendt tractor, a drill, a reversible plough, a fur-

Ellen, my mother, Vic and Sam.

row press, a new sprayer and a fertiliser spreader! We then did all our own work until 1995. When Victor decided he did not want to farm, and I was aware the pig unit wanted more money spent on it, plus the fact we had lost a fortune that year on pigs, and I had had a fire a year previously which just about knocked my end in, I decided to sell the pigs, get rid of all the machinery and go back to contracting again. Both Nick with twenty years service and Gary, who had been with me for three years as herd manager, found jobs immediately. We had a long discussion between us as to the reasons why I had taken the course I had and they quite understood.

Another important factor was that in 1985, I had replied to an advertisement in an arable paper called *English Farmer*, for someone to write about pigs. That was probably the most significant thing I have ever done.

I had always been interested in reading articles and columns written by farmers in any of the farming press, people like A. G. Street and Ralph Wightman, John Cherrington, and then latterly David Richardson. I first met David when I was very young and still active in Young Farmers. I thought then that he spoke a lot of sense and he has only improved over the years. He is indeed a very succinct writer.

I had always wanted to do something like that, even introduce the then farming programme on television. Well, we can all dream can't we? I did get involved for a while on local radio, but like television, farming programmes were deemed to be not very important and I suppose now that apart from BBC Radio 4's *Farming Today* programme in a morning, we have nothing left of any interest or relevance. I certainly don't think *The Archers* have anything to offer.

Inside everyone, I am sure there is a story waiting to be written. I had wondered time and time again, how I would ever get the opportunity to put my thoughts on paper. When I saw the advertisement in the *English Farmer* on that fateful Saturday morning, I knew something was going to come of it. I rang up immediately but of course being Saturday, no one could help me. I rang back on the Monday morning to be told that they had been inundated with replies, which didn't surprise me at all. I asked them what they actually wanted. They seemed unsure but thought perhaps I would like to write in describing my farm. I replied that I thought that would bore the pants off everyone and do me no favours at all, so eventually it was agreed that I could submit 'whatever I liked'.

I sat down and a bit tongue-in-cheek submitted about 500 words on how it taken me twenty years to start farming on my own account. I can still remember the first line and I repeat it here. 'Thu' disn't want owt wot eeats oot of a bag' said my ancient friend, when I told him that I had taken a farm and that pigs were to be a major part of it. I have often thought about his words and perhaps at times they have a ring of truth with them. Of course I was unable to type and my long hand isn't all that legible, so I asked the daughter of a local farmer, who did secretarial work, if she would type it for me. This she did with great aplomb and when I asked her how much I owed her, she said, 'If it is accepted, you can give me a kiss at Christmas'. The delightful girl, now a farmer's wife, can have as many kisses as she likes, as yes, it was accepted and ten days later I received a cheque through the post for £40.

There was a brief note from the editor, Digby Scott, stating that I had got the job, he liked what I had written and gave me the copy dates for the next nine issues. Panic set in. What on earth was I going to write about? At least it gave me something to think about as I went up and down fields on a tractor. No matter how skilled the job on a tractor, it can become a bit tedious, all except drilling. Drilling was always my favourite occupation, trying to take the nearest way across a field, that is to say, not to have any kinks in the rows of corn.

I need not have worried; inspiration always came. The half page became a page. At the end of the nine months, I rang up again to see if they wanted me to carry on, did they still like what I wrote or had they run out of money, as I had no further copy dates? I was somewhat surprised to find that the paper had been sold back to its original founder, Fred Noble, in Grimsby, who had sold it to the Lincolnshire Standard Group twenty years previously and he had become their advertising agent and boy, could he sell! I rang him up, told him I was the idiot who wrote the pig column. He asked which pig column so I said, 'The one in your paper'. Fred replied that he never looked at it, he only put it together. However, he did invite me over to 'discuss' the matter, took me to a very exclusive fish and chip restaurant, and then gave me the bill to pay. That was typical of Fred. He had a most warped sense of humour but was very clever. Prior to his advertising business, he had been a stand up comedian on the stage and was excellent at the ad libs and one liners. I took with me several of the previous columns I had written for him to read. He thought it was a good idea if I would carry on, but he could only afford £35! By this time, quite frankly, I was enjoying it so much, that I would have done it for 'nowt' as they say in Yorkshire.

I began to visit people to see what they were up to and why they were so successful at pig keeping. The page soon became two pages, then four pages and Fred said one day that it would be a good idea if I could get some advertising in to accompany what I had written. He felt it would help towards my travel expenses. By this time the tabloid *English Farmer* had become an attractive arable magazine, with my pig section in it and we had a circulation of some 14,000 readers in the Eastern Counties, many of them having pigs also.

In February 1987, Bernard Hoggarth of Cranswick Mill, rang me up to say that he thought I should start a proper pig magazine, instead of writing in an arable paper, as there was a niche in the market for the sort of idiotic rubbish I wrote. Thank you Bernard, the best thing you have ever said. He also added that I should make it interesting, provocative and if at all possible, amusing and that was all. Try to do something different from the magazines already on the market. Of course there was no point in copying anyone else, it really had to be a fresh start. To be honest, I wasn't all that keen to start with, as I was still very busy on the farm, working many hours as farmers do. However, Fred liked the idea, told me to get my backside through to Grimsby again to discuss the idea seriously. He made sure that I understood that although they had all the necessary facilities, he was far too busy to help in any way, so I would have to be responsible for both the editorial and advertising.

I went home again with a ringing in my ears. How on earth do you jump into a market, which was well subscribed already with magazines, and particularly from a cold start? Whom do you approach first? How much revenue did you need to get the first one off the ground? Where do you get circulation lists from and so on? I rang half a dozen people in the industry, whose advice I valued and much to my surprise they were all very enthusiastic and encouraging. It took me from February till June to get the first edition together. Ian Brisby of Newsham Pigs said he would take alternate front covers in the magazine for as long as we both wanted. This practice lasted until his company was liquidated and we were owed £3,000.

The first issue appeared in June 1987, neatly stapled inside *English Farmer*, as we had nowhere to send it to, other than the mailing list for that magazine. We included a reply paid card inviting people to respond if they were in pigs and would like to receive, what we hoped, would be a monthly issue for many years. We did the same thing the next issue. PIC [1] had kindly taken 3,500 copies of the first issue, so by the time we sent out the August issue we had nearly 5,000 names. At this point we deemed this sufficient to send out on its own.

The first issue inside *English Farmer* was very thick and heavy. It was printed in Liverpool and we had 17,500 printed. I persuaded a friend who had a Volvo Estate that he might like to come with me to collect them from Liverpool; I had ar-

1. Pig Improvement Company – the largest pig breeding company in the world.

ranged a visit to the Rolls Royce car factory on the way back
(a bit of diversion really, but what a trip) and he could be my
guest. We loaded up the Estate car and it looked as if the rear
end was on the floor it was so laden down. How we did not get
stopped by the police I know not. If ever any of you have the
opportunity of looking around the factory at Crewe, jump at
it. It was fascinating. Tom Jones was there, looking at his latest
car, which was due to be finished that day. It takes six weeks
from start to finish to produce a Rolls Royce, or at least it did
then, although I believe that may have changed since the factory has been modernised. One car had been out on test and
had been brought back upon its return. It was a left hand drive,
scheduled for the United States. Two engineers were scratch-
ing their heads so I asked if there was a problem. Apparently
the two separate air conditioning controls for the passenger
and the driver, were one degree out at one side!

On publication the magazine appeared to be well received,
people began telephoning with their problems and asking for
advice on certain pieces of equipment. The magazine grew in
stature. Digby Scott had resigned from his position in the Lincolnshire Standard Group and bought a half share in Fred's
company. He was still editing the *English Farmer* and was also
busy with his PR business. When Fred died several years later, Digby and his delightful wife Ann, bought the other half
of Fred's business and increased their PR work, after selling
English Farmer back to the Lincolnshire Standard Group, who
let it lie dormant for a while, before bringing it back as a tabloid. Digby has an acute brain, a wicked sense of humour, is
a wizard on computers and has the latest technology in the
publishing field.

Little did I know that when he sent me the first cheque for
£40 that would be the start of a lasting friendship, along with

a most satisfactory working relationship. To date, after meeting him twenty-one years ago, we have never had one wrong word. If anything needs to be discussed, that is exactly what happens. I never ask Digby and Ann what they are doing, they tell me, and they never ask me what I am doing or where I am going, but I always tell them. Without sounding conceited, I think I can safely say that *Pig World* has been a resounding success and surely ranks as the leading pig magazine today. It is a team effort, I stumble and fumble my way around the country and I suppose the world also. I try to find items of interest to pig farmers, and what goes on behind closed doors, and I invite the trade to spend money on supporting the magazine through advertising. Digby, in between his radio programme and his other many commitments, handles the layout of the magazine with whatever I want in it. He is brilliant at it. Ann helps on the advertising side and manages the invoicing and credit control. The arrangement seems to work.

It quickly became apparent to me that I would have to learn how to type. For the first few issues I managed to get that done for me, but when it moved to Grimsby, I thought I should buy a word processor. I did just that, and spent many an hour in front of it, listening to it making all those beeps, which meant I had got it wrong! Suddenly, I found I could use it quite effectively and what was really surprising was the fact that I actually enjoyed it. Well I say enjoy, I did unless I inadvertently erased a whole article before I had the chance to save it. That concentrates the mind quite sharply! Of course the next thing was to have a computer, which duly arrived. I taught myself how to use that to a limited degree, having been taught the basics by John Taylor of Tabrotec, a local farmer, who had diversified into computers, and from whom I had purchased the computer – in fact I have bought everything from John and he has been very patient.

Before long I needed an accounts package, a wages programme and all the other things you suddenly find are essential on a farm, like a pig recording scheme. All these things are
fine if you know how to get the most out of them, particularly
the pig recording. I have found since being involved in journal-
ism and visiting farms, that not everyone makes the most of
their records. Granted, they will churn out week after week,
how many pigs have done what and so on, but what they mostly fail to do is to utilise the information, or have the ability to
translate that information into a helpful form as to why the pigs
have not done what was budgeted for them to do. I see this time
and time again, and it is perhaps the one area that could have a
significant effect on the well-being of many units.

My children of course have been computer literate since
their first days at school. I well remember going along to the
village school when they first got a computer, an Apple Mac
or some such thing, which was set up for parents to try. Victor asked me to sit down, he was all of six at the time, and
explained what I had to do. It simply made a lot of rude noises
and the screen went blank. Victor shoved me to one side with
the words, 'Dad, don't you understand the first thing about
these wonderful machines, they are so simple?' He just sat
there as though he was playing a piano, and the screen dis-
played the most amazing things. I felt rather small.

I suppose this made me even more determined to master
modern technology. As time has progressed, I suppose I am
now reasonably capable of getting things done. The original
word processor was passed on to the family while Dad got a
brand new one. The next step was to update the computer so
that I could go 'surfing' and have email and all the other wonders of the cyber world. I have two different word processor
packages on the new one and now when I write an article, I

simply send it straight to Digby, so Ann no longer has to re-type my formerly faxed material as we now have the same software. It is absolutely wonderful and I am totally amazed! How on earth I ever managed previously, I simply do not know.

Farming in general and pig farming in particular has seen many changes in the time *Pig World* has been going and I am bound to say that we are to see even more in the future. Travel broadens the mind and in recent years I have travelled extensively not only in the United Kingdom but many overseas countries. How else would I have visited South Korea for example? How else would I have flown on a cargo Jumbo, where you live up in the cockpit with the crew, sit in the spare seat at take off and landing, and learn about the way aeroplanes fly? The latter was a fascinating trip, very tiring but what an experience. I drove down from Yorkshire early one morning to Tring in Hertfordshire, where we fed the 80 pigs due to fly out to Korea that evening. Each one was then individually examined by a vet who gave them a clean bill of health. Two lorries arrived to collect the pigs which were loaded in a specific order, as when they are loaded onto the plane, they are housed in specially built crates to hold either singles in the case of boars, or groups of gilts and they come off the lorry accordingly. Leaving Gatwick at eleven at night, we flew at 35,000 feet in a zig-zag path, first stop Dubai. One has to fly in such a fashion, as there are still areas that one is not allowed to fly over. Planes coming back the other way were flying 2,000 feet lower. It took six-and-a-half hours to reach Dubai, by which time it was nine-thirty in the morning and a bit on the warm side! Nevertheless, fresh fruit appeared to replenish our lockers, as well as food for the next stage to Hong Kong. That particular Cathay Pacific 747 freighter could get off the ground weighing 373 tonnes in total. The plane itself when empty of fuel weighs 140 tonnes and can carry 170 tonnes of fuel leaving room for about 60 tonnes of cargo. A Jumbo uses 10 tonnes of fuel per hour and a staggering 32 tonnes per hour equivalent when taking off. We carried a variety of cargo, spare parts, some lubricants, detergents, cloth, gold, machinery and of course the pigs. Cargo was delivered at Dubai and fresh cargo put on board. The pallets which carry the cargo are standardised throughout the world and the way the pallets are pulled into the plane's hold and moved within is a work of art.

The crew changed at Dubai who then took us on for another six-and-a-half hours, having had one-and-a-half hours on the ground, landing at Hong Kong at ten-thirty at night. I can vividly remember circling the airport at Hong Kong, which is surrounded by a range of horse shoe-shaped mountains which means the plane has to bank steeply before dropping quickly onto the runway, speeding towards the water at the other end, which from where I sat behind the captain, seemed to be getting a lot nearer very quickly. We slowed down sufficiently to turn at the end only about twenty metres from the edge. It was hot and humid. A generator was waiting for us so that cold air could be blown into the plane in order to keep the pigs cool. We were not to feed the pigs en route, but they did have water available. Each time the crew changed, they had to sign to say that the pigs had not been off the plane and that we had not taken on board any water for them. This was to satisfy the Koreans when we eventually arrived, as there is no country between Britain and Korea, which can be vouched for as free from foot and mouth disease.

Cathay Pacific have their headquarters in Hong Kong, so it was effectively the termination of the plane's round trip. It was thoroughly checked over again, more cargo put on and taken off, clean head rest covers on the seats, new food, and the plane hoovered out. Again, on the ground for 90 minutes, a new crew and off once more, this time to Taipei, the capital of Taiwan. A relatively short flight saw us landing there at one-thirty in the afternoon. A turn around time of 90 minutes seemed to be standard practice at all stops. When we left Gatwick, I was given a humane killer, in case I had to destroy a pig for whatever reason. Only I knew the combination of the box it was kept in and I was instructed not to tell the crew. This would not be allowed today.

Narita airport in Tokyo does not allow planes to land between midnight and dawn. As it was a three hour flight from Taipei, we actually landed bang on six, the first plane of the day. Everywhere else we had had one fork-lift type of vehicle to load and unload the cargo. Here we had four, very efficient. Although we had flown for many hours and had three stops, I still had to go through the safety checks, the Japanese are very thorough. What I could see of Japan from the air seemed to be neat and tidy and not an inch of ground wasted. Mount Fuji appears as a snow-clad arrowhead, rising up into the sky. It took another three hours to fly to Seoul, the capital of Korea and our final destination. It was hot, there was a cloudless sky, no fork lifts available, nothing to cool the pigs with, although it was not humid and they did not come to any harm. Eventually lorries appeared and we managed to get the five crates of pigs transferred to go a few miles down the road to the quarantine centre, which happened to be the same centre used the previous year for horses in the Olympic games. The pigs were unloaded and skipped down the concrete as if they had just travelled a couple of miles. We had actually been in the plane for about 32 hours and the pigs had not eaten for 48, but that did not seem to bother them, apparently they fly better on empty stomachs. Makes a mockery of the red tape certain organisations would love to impose on the transportation of animals overseas. The most stressful part of a journey for a pig at least is the loading and unloading, so no sense in the idea that pigs should be unloaded and rested after 12 or 24 hours or whatever the number of hours was suggested.

Having seen our charges loaded and leave the airport, Ian Goodbody, the Irish chap who had travelled with me from the breeding company and was taking some diluent for the artificial insemination centre which they had set up in Korea. Diluent in that form was a white powder in a glass bottle. The Koreans were almost paranoid about it, they thought we were smuggling drugs and I really thought they were going to lock us up. It was three days later before we were allowed to go back and collect the offending material.

Seoul is a fascinating city. Inhabited by around 12 million of their 42 million population, it is a city of two halves, the old and the new, separated by the river. Bearing in mind that the Olympics had been held there the previous year, lots of new hotels had been built and the city partially modernised. The Koreans are a very polite race. The girls are by-and-large extremely attractive, more than can be said for the men, but they always bow when they meet you. When I finally arrived at the Hilton Hotel at four-thirty Sunday afternoon, I was absolutely knackered. I had hardly slept at all. I went to my room, threw my case in a corner, dropped onto the bed and slept for a solid nine hours.

Since that first visit I have been back to Korea again flying with pigs for JSR Healthbred and to Thailand with a consignment for ACMC. [2] It is extremely pleasing and a compliment to British breeders that our stock is so sought after abroad and especially so in Asia.

2. Agricultural Contract Management Company who were the former National Pig Development Company.

10 | Asia

I had met some of the Koreans who were buying our pigs, when they had been over in Britain six weeks earlier, selecting their stock. One of them, aged about thirty, invited us, along with J. W. Kim, who had imported the pigs, to his luxury flat in Seoul one evening for a meal - and what a meal it was. He was a big player in farming generally, with unusually a large acreage, very uncommon in Korea, plus he had 1,500 sows, a fishing fleet and a merchant fleet. His children were being educated at a private school in Seoul, so they all lived there during the week, travelling out to the farm at weekends.

He had the most beautiful and amiable wife. We four men sat cross-legged on the floor round a low table, which after three hours becomes a very painful experience, I don't think I have ever been so uncomfortable. His wife brought in each course and there were eleven courses of the most exotic dishes, each with a different sauce, then she smiled sweetly, bowed and left the room each time. The children were ushered in, presented to us then banished. I realised then that Korea, like most other countries has a social divide. There is a lot of poverty there and you only need to drive a couple of miles down the road from Seoul and you literally go back a thousand years. Planting out rice in the paddy fields is a sight to behold, women working in water not quite up to their knees but well above their ankles. These women remind me now of the women I saw in Russia a year later inasmuch as they were five feet in all directions! Rice is the staple food of the Korean people and very important to them as a crop. One or two plantations had a sort of two-wheeled tractor to drive a rotavator whilst others still worked the paddy with bullocks. The more go-ahead farmers had actually supplied the women with yellow wellies, not the green ones we use. I saw crops I had never seen before like ginseng, which is supposedly an aphrodisiac (there are lots of things supposed to be, I have tried them all, none of them work!) exotic vegetables and fruits. It is quite common to drive through a small village or a town and find the natives or locals squatting on the pavements selling their produce.

I enjoyed Seoul, it is a vibrant city. Toll-roads built under private enterprise are a feature of South Korea. They are built wide enough so that planes could land on them, in case of another civil war and should the airport be damaged. We drove on one for 250 miles to Kwangu, the second city of the country and a University centre, for the cost of £8.50. It was here in the early 1980s where 2,000 students were shot for demonstrating. Coincidentally, our first night in Kwangu marked the anniversary of the uprising and the students were demonstrating again. They don't shoot them now, but there was a hell of a lot of soldiers about, all heavily armed. The streets were strewn with bricks hurled by the mob and we were advised not to poke our heads out of the hotel, as they would think we were Americans, and we might get bricks thrown at us. For some reason they do not like the Americans and they would not expect any English people to be there.

When visiting some of the units where the pigs were headed I had the opportunity to see a 3,000 sow herd, and also a couple of peasant farmers with only a few acres and maybe 30 or 40 sows. The buildings were built as if to take elephants but the engineered metal work inside was very flimsy and not really pig proof. The management of the herd was practically non-existent as we would know it, and Master Breeders, who were then selling pigs in Korea and had set up the AI stations, had also signed an agreement to supply management training along with nutritional expertise so as to capitalise on the supe-

Typical Korean pig unit.

rior genetics being sent. This I hasten to add was not an easy task when you had to point out to the stock people that the general idea was for boars to be mated with the gilts and the sows at the appropriate time, all very elementary.

It gets very hot in Korea, about ten degrees warmer than here and about ten degrees cooler in winter, which has some effect on the type of housing used. Pigs were allowed to roam outside from their intensive areas in pens that had shades pulled over them when very hot, aided by the addition of a sprinkler system. It was quite a mechanical achievement and good for the stock too. In between the rows of piggeries, trees had been planted to provide shade to the buildings.

On a couple of smaller units I came across what was called the blanket house. This consisted of a tubular steel frame, shaped a bit like an old nissen hut, which had a layer of insulation material rolled over the frame. On top of that was another layer, which was literally a blanket. This lasted for about five years and was simply replaced. In the summer, the material was rolled up at the sides to give ventilation and rolled down again in colder weather. It was exceedingly cheap to build. Nutrition at that time was a problem in Korea, particularly with the first stage rations, some of the pigs looking a bit on the impoverished side. I wanted to visit a slaughterhouse, but I never did. For some reason they were not keen for me to do that and I suspect that things were perhaps not all they should be. Certainly when I saw some of the meat on sale in the back streets of Seoul, it rather confirmed my suspicions.

It is now seventeen years since I went and at that time they had 650,000 sows. It was their intention to double the size in three years. I believe that they have managed to get to around 950,000. I worked out that if they increased their herd to the original target, they would need another three million tons of imported feed, and they are but one of a number of Far Eastern countries who are doing the same thing. They love pork and as soon as a country begins to become prosperous, they increase pork consumption, either by importing it or producing it. Although at the time of writing, we cannot sell our grain at anywhere near the cost of production, if all the developing countries were to increase their herd and want extra feedstuffs there would simply not be enough to go round. That could lead to an interesting situation. I have often thought the next war will be about food. At the moment there are no surplus world supplies to mean anything and if every person in China wanted to eat one kilo more of pork, there is insufficient available for us to do that, so does that mean in the long run the future of agriculture is reasonably safe?

The South Koreans really are the most hospitable people on earth. I flew back to Seoul from Kwangu and as we landed, we had to pull all the blinds down in the plane as we were not allowed to see the fortifications around the airport, in case we were North Korean spies. Of course I had already seen them when I first landed, as no such instructions were forthcoming on the freighter Jumbo. They are paranoid about North Korea. In the civil war in the 1950s, South Korea suffered heavy casualties and the whole of their beautiful country was damaged and the vegetation all burnt off by Napalm bombs. This meant that at the time I was there, none of the fresh green and lush trees and bushes were older than thirty-five years. Korea is 75% mountains, the remainder being very fertile valleys. Labour is of course very cheap, which is probably why they maintained a subsistence form of farming. With their current economic difficulties, I guess farming has not advanced much and it makes me feel that perhaps for some time, it will not progress far beyond the peasant state.

They were very big in shipbuilding at the time, and car manufacturing was a growth area. The Koreans are brilliant engineers, as seen by their roads and dams, ships and cars, and their engineering tool manufacturing. In Seoul itself, which is a bustling city twenty-four hours a day, it is quite common to find a row of what looks like lock-up garages down a street, but each will house a small business, mostly engineering. Of course our Health and Safety would have a field day, as there is no protection whatsoever for the workers.

Flying back to Seoul from Kwangu, I was met at the airport by Jinny Kim, a twenty-four year-old student studying languages and the daughter of J. W. Kim. She virtually ran her father's business and spoke perfect English. She had set the day aside so that she could take me sightseeing and to look around the shops. She would not let me pay for any of the meals at all, in fact I think she was offended because I offered. I had a really good look at everything, including going up their tallest building and having a panoramic view of the city. I was then put on a plane bound for Hong Kong where I was to spend a couple of days.

There is a buzz of excitement in Hong Kong. The name Hong Kong means fragrant garden. I called it Hong Pong, which is self-explanatory. It was very, very humid. I landed at approximately six-thirty in the evening. I immediately changed my Korean dollars into American dollars, hailed a taxi to take me to the Kowloon Hotel. He asked me for the equivalent of £2.50 in dollars but in my haste and naivety, I gave him the equivalent of £20 saying that was OK. He disappeared very quickly before I realised my mistake! Air conditioning is a must in Hong Kong. All hotels and restaurants had it, as had taxis, coaches and even the underground. This made things worse when you emerged into the outside world, it was like walking into a brick wall and if you have never experienced heat of this nature it is quite incomprehensible.

I cautiously walked the streets, feeling my way around. What a fascinating place, it hums with life, all sorts of life all the time, I really don't think it ever stops. There are some superb restaurants, lots of clubs and gambling dens; gambling is a Chinese pastime, the likes of which I have never seen elsewhere. On every street corner there is someone waiting to relieve you of your dollars for wine, cameras, jewellery, or for having a suit made. I opted for a suit, three shirts and three silk ties, all for £160. The suit was measured at nine-thirty in the morning, I went for a fitting later that afternoon, and collected the finished article the next morning! It fitted perfectly, the shirts were all double stitched, and my initials were embroidered on their pockets. That suit fitted me for five years before I 'outgrew' it.

It is understandable that a lot of vice and crime are part of the make up of Hong Kong. I had three trips onto Hong Kong Island, once by the famous Star Ferry from Kowloon, which cost five pence, once on the underground, which cost fifty pence and once in a taxi that cost £5. There literally is not a spare inch on the island. Skyscrapers abound, very near to each other. I visited an open market that was held in a purpose built arcade or building and I have never in all my life experienced anything quite like it. Fish in tanks and poultry in cages were everywhere. You told the trader which chicken or duck you wanted and he simply cut its head off and gave it to you. Similarly with fish, you made your choice and it was pulled out of the tank. Blood was everywhere, the noise was almost unbearable. There was every conceivable item of food you could think of plus several you would not. Hygiene did not exist at all. The squalor in the Chinese living quarters I will never forget, whilst the splendour of the 'white' residences up the hill are equally as impressive. It is definitely a mixed social structure. I would like to have gone to mainland China, to Aberdeen Harbour and to Sun Valley, the race course, but time just did not permit any of these activities.

There seemed to be a deal of unrest on the Saturday before I left late at night. Little did I realise then that the next morning the Tianamen Square uprising would take place, which had such dramatic effects for the future of not only Hong Kong but the whole of China. I was very fortunate to leave when I did. Having flown out on a freighter and feeling part of the plane so to speak, I found flying back as a 'normal' passenger so boring. I had bought a Jeffrey Archer novel in Hong Kong airport and as I landed at Gatwick, after touching down at Bahrain for ninety minutes, the full thirteen hours of flying had enabled me to read it from cover to cover, the last chapter finished as the wheels touched the tarmac.

That meant I had not slept for quite a while, in fact all of Saturday plus the travelling time. I was met by taxi and taken back to Tring, where I then had to drive back to Yorkshire. I don't know how I kept awake, probably by calling at every Little Chef for coffee.

I suppose once you travel it gets in your blood. Less than a year later, I was off again, this time to Russia, or perhaps more accurately, the Ukraine, the former bread basket of Europe.

PIC had an agreement to restock a 3000 sow unit in the Ukraine. I took a phone call from them one day enquiring as to whether I would be interested in accompanying a consignment of gilts and boars to this unit. A silly question really!

At that time my mother was on her death bed, having had a stroke from which she was never to recover. I rang my sister to see what I should do and she persuaded me to go saying that mother would want me to go, and if she died while I was away, they would keep her on ice till I returned! Ever the practical sister. In the event, my mother died the day after my return. The hospital she was in was on the way home from Humberside Airport, so I called in on the way back. She still looked exactly as she had done when I left, and even though she was unconscious, when I spoke to her to tell her I was back, she squeezed my hand. She had had a hard life in many ways and both my sister and I will be eternally grateful to her for the unselfish devotion she gave to both of us, not only that but her grim determination, her sense of fair play, her wit and humour, her love of her four grandchildren, her flair for gardening, all these memories of her will remain with us for our life times. Those of you who have lost a mother will know of the tremendous gap they leave.

The two lorry-load of pigs had travelled down from Aberdeen on a Saturday, stayed overnight at the PIC Boroughbridge site and then been driven to Hull on the Sunday morning. I met the lorries on the docks in Hull, where I saw them board the Russian ship, which at that time brought all the Lada cars

Sam on way to Ukraine with breeding stock from PIC, 1990.

to Britain. They were to spend four days onboard, before they reached Leningrad as it then was, now St. Petersburg. I didn't really fancy bouncing about on the North Sea for that period of time, so flew out of Humberside to Amsterdam, three days later, where I boarded an Aeroflot whatever it was, for the flight to Leningrad. I quickly realised that the airline should be called Aeroflop! It was horrendous. The meal was terrible, the plane was filthy and there was a bullet hole in the locker above my head. Normally I find air stewardesses attractive. In this case, the poor girls wore very heavy make-up that matched their stature and their very thick uniforms. They were more like soldiers than stewardesses! The plane arrived in one piece at the old airport in Leningrad, as the new one was still under construction. I waited almost an hour and a half before my suitcase eventually arrived and I swear it had been opened. Getting through customs was the next hazard and that too seemed to last forever. I had been tannoyed in Amsterdam airport, to the effect that the two girls who were supposed to be meeting me at the airport in Leningrad would be late as the Aeroflot plane from Kiev to Leningrad had not turned up. I had instructions to take a taxi to the hotel where they would pick me up the next morning. Sarah was an American girl working for PIC on the unit and Natasha was the interpreter. The taxi job to the hotel was a bit of a free for all, and I was approached by a man who looked a bit like the Mafia! Did I want a taxi? I showed him the address of the hotel and he ushered me towards a piece of metal on four wheels which twenty-five years earlier had been a Lada. We set off with the driver leaning across into the passenger seat, his windscreen had so many large cracks in at the driver's side, so as to be completely opaque. It would not go into top gear and the noise from the engine, gear box and transmission would do a space rocket credit. Without any warning, right in the middle of Leningrad, the driver stopped and said in very good English, 'You give me money now'. I said sure, how many roubles do you want? I thought he was going to have a heart attack when I mentioned roubles, as he desperately wanted dollars. I agreed he could have dollars and when I eventually arrived at the rather splendid looking floating hotel, I asked him how many dollars he wanted. He replied, 'Twenty-five'. I did not have any five dollar bills and he did not have any change, so he grabbed the thirty dollars I had tendered and shot off in a cloud of black smoke. Next day Sarah asked me how much the taxi had cost and when I told her she laughed and said that I could have hired one all week for that sort of money! It reminded me of my episode in Hong Kong the previous year.

The hotel was quite acceptable except the telephones did not work. In fact I could not phone home for the full week I was away. The receptionist did not speak English and my one term of Russian at school was by no means sufficient to hold a conversation with him either. I gave my name he shook his head and said, 'Niet'. I tried PIC, again the negative, so in desperation I showed him a copy of *Pig World* and he beamed and said something like 'Da'. Apparently I had been booked in as *Pig World*.

Five the next morning a knock on my door heralded the arrival of Sarah and Natasha who had eventually flown up during the night. We were due to meet the ship at ten-thirty that morning and it took Natasha two hours to get permission for me to go onto the docks. The office that she rang was only a mile away, but it took nearly thirty minutes for her to get through on the phone, and you think we have problems!

The ship duly arrived, I was given lunch, at least I think it was lunch, on the ship and then we set to, to get the lorries off the ship so that we could get away to start the long drive down to the Ukraine. But it was not as easy as that, red tape abounded. The pigs, which were in partitions of eight on the lorries, and trailers, had to be completely mucked out and a special lorry arrived to take the muck away for incineration. There followed a disinfection programme the likes of which you have never seen, before the lorries were allowed off the ship. The remaining sawdust and shavings were also taken away and the pigs were bedded up with wet wood chippings, which had been brought up on a lorry from the unit in the Ukraine. There was also a large water bowser in tow, which was to carry the feed that we had brought with us. The reason for the lorry was that there was nowhere we could pick up fresh water between Leningrad and our destination!

Believe it or not but it was late afternoon before we actually left the docks. Driving through the centre of Leningrad at rush hour was like driving through a ghost town, very few vehicles about. It is a large city, a city of many contrasts, some beautiful buildings and monuments with statutes next to crumbling apartment blocks. The road we took was supposedly the main route from Leningrad down through Belarus to the Ukraine and equivalent in importance to our M1. It was hellish. The surface was awful, having been laid by women mainly, with tarmac in barrows, and levelled by hand rake without any substructure to it. It began to rain, which did not improve matters much. The countryside in Russia was bloody awful, drab, like the people, scrubby sort of bushes and small trees, sandy looking land, poor crops, lots of weeds, hovels for people to live in, and generally quite depressing.

There are no cafés or restaurants en route, nowhere to get a cup of tea, no toilets and no fuel pumps either. We had a hell of a job to get diesel, we had to borrow some coupons from the Russian lorry driver, who eventually in the early hours of one morning managed to find a pump in some back street of a god-forsaken village.

We travelled the first evening until one in the morning. By then the rain was so heavy we literally could not see, so we pulled up in a lay-by to get some sleep. During the night somebody hammered on the driver's door of the lorry. John, the driver, was a bit of a hard nut I reckon and after ascertaining that the fellow wanted dollars for ten times the going rate, so desperate was the need for currency, he told him to Sodoffski, or something offski! It was very effective or so we thought at the time. However, when daybreak came we found that this chap or perhaps one of his accomplices had taken the sheet that covered the feed, and the rain had reduced the paper sacks to tissue paper. This made it difficult for us to feed the pigs, it was like juggling with porridge! The pigs were fed every day and watered three times. Eventually when we took them off the lorries they had been on for eight days. How did they travel you might ask just as though they had gone a hundred yards down the road? All this modern legislation about unloading and resting is the biggest load of nonsense. Pigs travel very well and the breeding companies make sure they are not overstocked.

I had an HGV licence, so was able to take a turn at the wheel, which meant that the three of us were able to keep the two lorries going. Which we did, apart from the first night, the watering of the pigs and the inevitable brew up at the side of the road, along with any call of nature usually answered by a visit to some bushes at the roadside! We had to follow the lorry from the unit and whose driver was absolutely crazy. He went through lights at red, whipped across level crossings at red, in fact he was a complete lunatic. He drove there and back apparently without any sleep aside from the first night. When we eventually arrived at Checkassey his eyes were bloodshot.

Two modern lorries amongst the ancient heaps driven there obviously drew a lot of attention. We were stopped three times by police who were being a bit nosy. Once while having a break we were approached by a man in a rather swish BMW who claimed to have a pig farm in another one of the satellite states, and was interested in buying pigs. Other lorry drivers flocked around our lorries almost in awe.

Some 1000 miles later, we arrived at the unit. As it was a Saturday and no one was about we went to bed until nine the next morning and was I glad to see a bed.

Different people have differing ideas about what constitutes a vet. Some of the vets on the unit were no more than ordinary stockmen. The head vet who had a twenty-five year-old Moskavich that was his pride and joy, carefully watched the pigs being unloaded. One gilt happened to have a few more hairs than the others, so he was convinced it had pneumonia, whilst another gilt with a bit of concrete burn was deemed to have bone disease. We managed to persuade him, with the help of the superb Natasha, that all was well so the pigs were driven into their new quarters. If we had the same conditions here in Britain we could well be in trouble. The unit was a massive sprawling complex, built as if to house hippos, but not very welfare friendly. The individual buildings were very high, so consequently very cold. I didn't like it at all, and that was after PIC had persuaded them to make many alterations. I know the agreement included a three year management period as the basic stockmanship was non-existent. Simple things like planning service, having a regular flow of production were almost beyond the comprehension of the locals.

The service passages to the sections of the unit, which were 500 metres long, were also centrally heated and that was just for the staff to walk through. Some 182 personnel worked or at least put in an appearance on the unit. There is no such thing as unemployment. I remember looking in one piggery where one man sat on a chair, watching the cogs turn round on the automatic feeding system, while another stood at the outlets to make sure that the meal actually came out, and then a third had a hose pipe to water the feed in the troughs. I don't think it took longer than half-an-hour to complete their task and that was their days' work done.

Nutrition was another problem area. Although there was a fairly new state-of-the-art feed mill, capable of producing 120,000 tonnes per year, ingredient availability left a lot to be desired. One day they would have no wheat, next day there would be no protein. The idea of the unit, a former collective farm, was that it would provide the breeding stock for the other collective farms in the area. Prior to the arrival of PIC, the stock on all the units was the old Estonian sows, which were very large, very fat and not at all prolific. I shudder to think what the probe would be, probably somewhere in the 30 range. Growth rates were awful, at least a year for a pig to reach 120 kilos.

Conditions on these units for the staff were quite good in Russian terms. Each family had a house with a hectare of land. On this they grew their own food or as much as they could. If they wanted to sell it, that was fine too. They were not paid very much, and the local shops had very little to offer other than cabbages and tomatoes. Fashion was non-existent, luxuries were few and far between, and the way houses were built had to be seen to be believed. Windows did not fit, walls were not straight, doors did not always close, ceilings and floors were not even, electric wiring was a joke and where I stayed, there was no water in the upstairs bathroom. The roads outside the houses were not made up, the whole place looking like a bomb site. The only well built, tidy looking place apart from the Italian designed feed mill, was the kindergarten. Children were sent there as young as one, if not younger, so mothers could go back to work. They have free education and medicine and the children were taught from the outset that they were the luckiest people on earth and they must not envy the decadent West. I did have the opportunity of visiting several other units and found them to be similarly designed and managed. They were not happy that I was taking photographs, particularly when there were litters of pigs of two in number only!

I always thought that the Russians had no sense of humour. True mostly, but Gregor, the assistant manager on the unit, told me several stories that poked fun at his fellow countrymen, then fell on the floor laughing like mad.

One of Gregor's stories was about the fact that there were no garages in the Ukraine with showrooms where you could walk in and buy a car. Very few of the peasants had cars, and those that had should have been banned. There were several motor cycles though, quite a popular mode of transport with four or more people on board. If someone felt they could justify a car, they could order one from the Lada factory for delivery in eight years time!

To continue with Gregor's story, apparently one of the locals ordered a car and was told it would take the normal eight years. He asked if it would be possible to have it delivered in July. He was told that it couldn't and they wouldn't guarantee it. So he pleaded that if it could he would like it on 6 July. Why so precise came back the reply? Because said our friend, it will be my silver wedding on that day and I would like it as a present for my wife. He was then told that they would see what they could do but again wouldn't promise, so he stuck his neck out again and said well if you can't do it on that day, can you deliver it in the afternoon? Exasperated by now he was asked why the afternoon and he replied, 'Well, we have a leak and the plumber has promised to come that morning!'

The second story concerned pig production. It is not uncommon to find a typical Russian sow with only two piglets. Gregor told me that a man on a unit came to work one morning to find that a sow had had only two piglets. Everything in Russia has to be recorded, but he was a bit reluctant to put two on the sheet, so he wrote four instead. He then took the sheet to his immediate superior who changed the figure to eight piglets. By the time the sheet reached Moscow the sow had been credited with twelve piglets. A meeting of the Soviet was called in the Kremlin where the man responsible for agriculture proudly told his colleagues that in the Ukraine there was a very prolific sow. It had twelve pigs and as their neighbours in Poland were very poor, wouldn't it be a nice gesture if they gave them two piglets and kept the ten themselves!

I have no idea where I would want to live other than Britain. I saw that the Ukraine had much to offer inasmuch as the soil was magnificent with enormous potential, but seventy years of being overshadowed by communism had knocked the stuffing out of the locals and they were in no way able to take advantage of that potential, nor in fact did they have the desire to do so. The younger generation were beginning to realise that all was not well and that a greater opportunity existed outside their mother country. Achieving some of that though was not easy for them, but they were loathe to accept the then current methods. I am not for one minute suggesting that I would want to live there, but give me a thousand acres of their soil any day.

It was somewhat depressing to see the thin, weed-infested crops, the crappy old machinery and totally inefficient way of doing things. They had no fertiliser or sprays, and no technology. Yet having said that, a part of the area was set aside as a Ukrainian museum with the housing, clothing and customs all on show with tremendous pride. Perhaps the new generation of farmers will alter things, provided they can get hold of some greatly needed capital.

All in all I had a most interesting week trying to discover what makes the Russians tick. I came to the conclusion that it was not a lot! Not sure what the punishment was for crime, but the unit was completely surrounded by a security fence, to prevent the workers from stealing the pigs to take home to eat. Several of the workers did have the odd pig in their gardens, don't ask me where they came from, and it was a nightmare as the powers-that-be had to try and get rid of them from a health hazard point of view. Other than those local pigs, the next unit was quite some distance away.

Believe it or not when I ate in the canteen on the unit special food was brought in just for me, so that I would think that they all lived well. Most of the time I had no idea what I was eating but it was prepared with great ceremony.

It was with a great feeling of sadness that I left the unit in the early hours one morning for the two hour drive to Kiev airport. I need not have worried about missing the plane, again it had not turned up and the worst thing was that nobody knew where it was or if it even existed. Four hours later it arrived without explanation. I flew to Prague with the thought that at least the delay had cut down my waiting time at Prague airport. Want to bet? Unbelievably, good old British Airways was also a couple of hours late. So there I was, no 'proper' currency having been advised not to take credit cards as they were sure to be nicked! A film was showing in an ante-room about the delights of Prague, so I watched it three times. Eventually the Boeing 737 arrived and an hour-and-a-half later I was safely delivered to Heathrow, where I was just in time to catch the flight back to Humberside. I couldn't help noticing the contrast between here and where I had just flown from as I gazed down upon the rows and rows of thick straw swaths in neat orderly lines, and the particularly tidy farms of Lincolnshire which hosts our local airport.

That year was certainly a year of travel. I had been in Germany earlier and met a couple of chaps from the United States, one of whom was into shared managed units in a big way, and the other who professed to run what was to be the world's largest abattoir. A gushing invitation from both made me think, and two months after my visit to Russia I took the whole fam-

Niagara Falls, 1990.

ily to America for mine and the children's first ever visit. Ellen had been in 1964 on a YFC exchange visit and had kept in touch with one particular farming family. We flew from Heathrow to Philadelphia, picked up a car and set off right at rush hour in that very busy city.

After a couple of hours driving, having been on the go for more than eighteen hours, we all felt the need of some sleep. We were immediately amazed at how cheap both food and accommodation were, at least half the price of what we would pay back home. When it came to filling up the car, it cost something like £7! We must be the most over-taxed country in the world.

We made our way to Niagara Falls, a sight to be seen at least once I think, and yes, they are big but not as impressive as the Victoria Falls. I was reminded of the two Americans I had seen at the Victoria Falls who had commented to each other that Victoria made Niagara look like a drop of sweat! Perhaps that was over-stating the situation, but I knew what they meant. Victoria is a mile wide and a deeper gorge. Following a line along the bottom edge of the Great Lakes, passing through Buffalo, Erie, Cleveland and Toledo, we saw a fair cross section of different aspects of American farming. Our trip was around about the time of Halloween and I have never in my life seen so many pumpkins, they were everywhere. Maize harvest was about to begin and it really was a sight to see the massive grain silos that seemed to be reaching for the skies.

Our destination was to be Brookville in Indiana, having first to visit the two gentlemen who had invited us to see them at work. One visit was very successful and I was able to see how he carried out his operation from supplying the feed, to arranging markets for the hogs. I was intrigued by the design of the piggeries. They obviously have greater extremes of climate than we do. The tractors on the farms, the cars they drove and the lorries were absolutely enormous. The livestock lorries were mostly possum-bellied ones, giving a lower deck between the tractor wheels and the articulated wheels, above which there would be another three decks. We had to stop at

Large possum-bellied livestock lorry, Indiana.

a rail crossing once and I swear the train which went past that was full of new cars, must have been at least a mile long.

The visit to the abattoir didn't really take place. Yes, I found it and arrived there on time. Unfortunately, the abattoir opening had been delayed due to strikes by the workers and the water supply had not been connected. The man we were supposed to see met me briefly, apologised for his soon to be absence as he had to see his 'attorney' about what to do with the strikers. At least I saw the world's largest abattoir from a distance!

We arrived in Brookville a day ahead of schedule to a tremendous welcome from the Bruns family. They have four sons and three daughters, all but one living in the vicinity. Three of the boys farm so I had a great week looking round their very different operations. All kept 'hogs' in various ways. One had improved genetics in his stock, another had the traditional multi-coloured, very fat pigs, probably crosses between Hampshire and Duroc with a peculiar blend of local breeds thrown

Fat pigs in an abbatoir, Indiana

in for good measure. We actually visited an abattoir one day to see some of the pigs killed. They were not only varied in colour, but also in size and were as fat as butter and when hung up looked like bullocks! Grading then was not a feature, it was just so many cents per pound irrespective, unless the carcase was under 100 kilos, then you were penalised. The abattoir was old, very labour intensive and has since closed.

I had my first experience of harvesting maize, or corn as it's called in the United States. I decided it was very hard on the combines and that our Health and Safety Executive would have had a field day. No guards on machinery, two loaded unbraked trailers being pulled behind one tractor. That sort of thing, nothing seemed to matter and they never came to any harm. I did ask what work was carried out in the growing of maize and was told, apparently very little inasmuch as it can be grown on the same land each year, doesn't get disease, just needs plenty of manure and as this crop was genetically modi-

Large tractor with discs, Indiana.

fied, it didn't even need the stem weevil spray. I thought that was good so perhaps we need to look more closely at GM without all the hysteria.

The pig industry has changed considerably in Britain since then but probably more so now in the United States. Most of our breeding companies have a stake in genetics over there, either directly or on a franchised basis. I did wonder at one time what would happen to our European market and that in the Far East also, if the United States who then had 10 million sows, ever got their act together from a production and marketing side of things. I now know! They have the ability to produce very cost-effectively because of the availability of cheap maize and soya. They do not yet have the restrictions placed upon them regarding slurry and planning as we do, but it will come and they do have a lot more mechanisation. One thing they do not have is the welfare of the pig at heart and stockmanship leaves a lot to be desired. Because the units are new, they are not likely to want to change them for at least twenty years, so welfare is not an issue for them. I would have thought that as we are subject to stringent welfare practices, and as we are led to believe retailers want welfare friendly produce, that that would cut down their marketing options, but mark my word, money talks and if they can produce pig meat cheap enough someone somewhere will buy it, irrespective of all the considerations.

I went back to the United States seven years later. Things had changed dramatically, but still the stockmanship angle bugged me. It was as I discovered a numbers game keeping pigs. It would appear at first sight that the more the merrier so far as sow numbers go, and seemed to be the norm. I was asked on one unit what I thought about the layout. I suggested they had too few farrowing spaces as they had done away with

Maize silos.

the boars and were using AI. That meant they had room for an extra 200 sows in the old boar pens. The remainder were in stalls, what else? So they had gone from 1350 sows to 1550 still with 264 crates. They said that would not be a problem, they would simply wean the pigs at fourteen days (illegal over here) and that would give them an extra 100 pigs per week. I said that perhaps they would not get the sows in pig again so easily as the uterus is not ready at fourteen days, so perhaps they would produce 100 pigs per week less. In that case came the reply, we will simply keep more sows!

It is a fact that the United States now, with eight million sows, are producing more pigs than they used to do with ten million. I can't help but think that our improved genetics have had a fair bit to do with that.

Everything is big there, the country itself, the things they have and they do have a wonderfully laid back attitude to life, there does not appear to be any stress at all, but there surely must be?

I had only been back home from the United States for a couple of weeks when I had the opportunity to go to the VIV [1] show

---

1. Company based in the Netherlands that organizes livestock shows in Asia, China, Europe and Latin America.

in the Netherlands. I set off with two friends and after we had done the show it was decided we would visit a unit in East Germany, where we had a contact, because of a steward on North Sea Ferries whom the other two knew very well. His name was Fred and had come from the Netherlands originally and settled in England after marrying a local girl. That meant we had to ring home to say that instead of being back on such and such a day, it was possible we would be delayed by four days or so; always a difficult one that.

It was a hell of a long way up through the Netherlands into West Germany via Munster, Osnabruck, Bremen, Hamburg and Lubeck, before passing through the deserted border posts, as the wall had come down exactly a year earlier, and travelling on to Rostock. That was some journey and I did not take kindly to the German driver of a sporty BMW who whilst we were travelling at the maximum of 142 mph insisted on driving tight up to our rear bumper, whilst flashing his lights for us to get out of his way, which when we were able to do he drove past giving us the V sign disappearing as though we were standing still.

What a contrast between East and West. Everything, which was good and well built, was in the West. The exact opposite was so apparent in the East with the exception of some lovely old houses going back to when Germany was as one previously. The roads were awful, the cars were the old Wartburg or Trabant, everywhere looked grey and drab which reminded me of my recent trip to Russia. Huge blocks of flats were being built but they were not well constructed. No service roads had been provided and the inhabitants were sprawling about in mud on their way home again. We discovered one excellent hotel, a joint venture with Sweden, where we found a crowd of West Germans with their wives who were dripping in jewellery. The car park was full of the élite of German motors and it was obvious they were on the lookout to make some money from the emerging Eastern sector. Car firms were beginning to move in with grass fields as sites and a tent for a showroom.

We visited Fred's sister, whom we later found out had given us all her food and left herself with nothing. Such was the kindness of those people. My heart went out to them, as they had very little. There was no nightlife for them, no entertainment of any kind, very few television sets and what we found amazing was the fact that they could not get used to being 'free'. When we later visited the pig unit, the staff kept looking over their shoulders as if to make sure that nobody was watching. We asked the unit manager if he had been to the VIV show and he said no, he hadn't realised he could go without permission. It was very strange indeed. The unit was for 3,000 sows and had previously been a communal farm. There was some difficulty about actual ownership and no one knew who owned the land the unit stood on. The workers had been more or less given the unit but had no capital with which to run it and as there could be no such thing then as unemployment, all the staff had been kept on and was selling off the sows to pay the wages. Previously to the Berlin Wall coming down they had supplied Poland with their pig meat at around eleven Ostmarks per kilo. Once the West took over, they decided they would eat the meat themselves but only paid 2.5 Deutchmarks per kilo. That decision also had an effect on the British market at the time as we export a considerable amount to Germany.

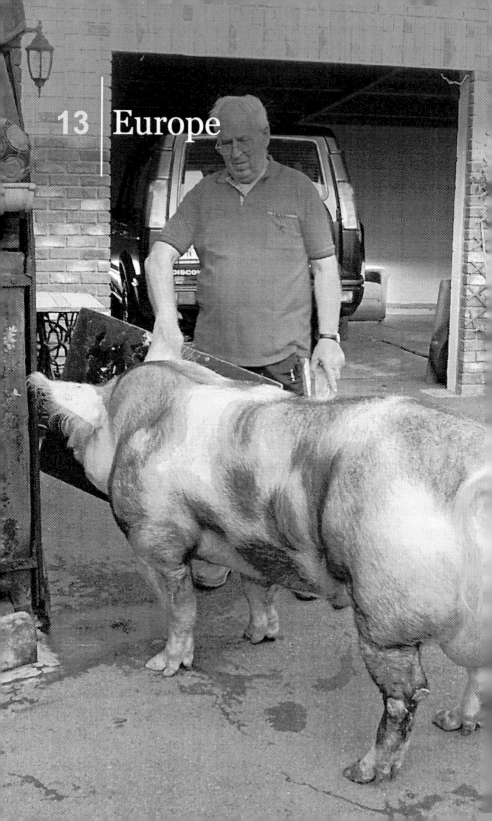

Since that trip, I have been back to Europe many times. No matter how many times I go, I never cease to wonder at how we are so different, or can it be they that are different? It always appears that agriculture is important to other European countries, as the farmers seem to be well looked after. I really believe that no matter which political party is in power here that farming to them is a nuisance and they really don't give a damn. I think they believe that somewhere out there is Utopia, which will provide all the food we want at a ridiculously low price.

Normally, all through my farming life, there has always been some enterprise in the industry that would give a decent return, provided you followed the rules of good husbandry. Currently no matter what rules you apply, there is nothing left at the end. This cannot be allowed to continue. Prosperous farming means a prosperous country and countryside. To get an indication of the state of affairs one only needs to look in the local papers at the ever increasing numbers of receiverships across a whole range of industries, many of which are allied to farming. We have had redundancies in the machinery trade, the feed mills, and service industries to farming. Even shops in my local towns of Beverley and Driffield are reporting a steadying in trade as the farming fraternity have stopped spending. When things become hard, farmers tighten their belts another notch and do stop spending, even on essentials in some cases and many feel they cannot afford to carry out even the basic rules of agronomy or stockmanship. Some examples would be not to put an essential spray on which would be cost effective, as they haven't the money to buy them in the first place, and on the stock side, troughs with holes in, or the leaking water tank, are not repaired as it costs money but not as much as it saves. It may be false economy but bank borrowings and high interest rates are not the farmer's favourite scenario. There are many additives for feed, which certainly enhance cost effectively the growth rate or general performance of animals. In hard times these are omitted and will eventually be banned. There are several products for putting into slurry and manure to reduce smell and improve the quality of the product. When money is tight, these are the first things to go out of the window, so the rural economy is vital for a host of other suppliers.

We hear about our competitors being given financial aids in various forms but the poor old British farmer has to plod on, on top of all the rules and regulations that others don't seem to have. You know there is an old adage that you should live today as if you were to die tomorrow and farm today as if you would live forever. Traditionally some farmers have been able to do that but currently there is no pleasure in farming and precious little in other aspects of life, no wonder farming rates has one of the highest suicide risks.

Many years ago, or perhaps not so many years ago, provided the jobs or routine work on a farm was done in the way we had been taught, that is good basic husbandry skills, the end result was acceptable. Now the industry is full of 'advisers' who set targets, which in turn cause stress and stress is a killer. There was never any stress when I was younger, you simply worked off any aggression and you certainly didn't need to go to a gymnasium or pump iron! Things have changed dramatically and will no doubt continue to change as nothing is forever, but I do believe we have left behind a rather satisfying period in farming. At one time, farms were alive, men were about, but when some of today's new farm management groups boast that they can farm 900 acres with one man, and are trying to stretch it to 1,000 acres, I believe that leaves a lot to be desired. I am not against progress, but I am not sure that this is progress.

If I look at pig farming in Western Europe and the United States as an example, they have many more sows per man than we can manage. I ask myself why that is and the answer is simple. We are better stockmen and are not fully automated and we do have welfare regulations not always seen elsewhere. If a pig farmer goes to a bank and asks for money to build a piggery, he might get it, certainly wouldn't at this moment in time, and if he did, it would have to be paid back in five years or not a lot longer. In Holland or Denmark, the answer would be cer-

Sam with staff of an Austrian farm.

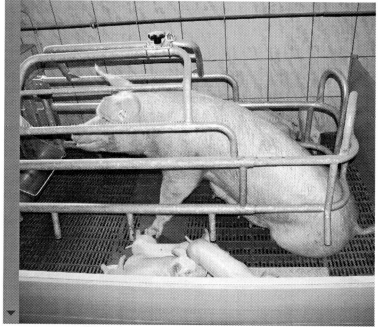

Very hygienic Austrian piggery.

tainly and take it over twenty-five years, at a reduced or very low interest rate.

Again in the nostalgic past, once we had produced whatever product we worked on the farm it seemed that our responsibility for that product ended as the lorry left the farm gate. The recent downturn in prices makes me question that these days, for the criteria has to be first of all obtain a market for your product before you serve a sow or sow a grain. The problem we have though is that there are too many anomalies now and products can be spun up for all sorts of reasons never heard of years ago. Take malting barley as an example. You would take a sample to the local market where several representatives from competing companies would look at it, sniff it, then bite it and say it is worth so much and they would honour that. Now a chap comes with a spear, prods about in the bin or in the heap of corn, takes a sample away and it is then put through the most amazing number of tests which are pretty meaningless to a grass roots farmer, only to come out with the fact that it is only worth a couple of quid above feed because of this, that, or the other, and sure as hell when you send the actual load in, it is even worse than the test said. I have had this happen to me twice. The first time I accepted what they said and took a lower price even though it still went for malting. The next time the load had been taken up to Edinburgh and I received a phone call to say that it would not pass for malting and would I take a lower price? I said no, if it is not what you said it was at first, and you tested it, then you can bring it back at your expense. It suddenly got through at the brewery, so don't give in too easily, and keep samples.

A friend of mine once said to me that there are two things farmers should do on any farm and that is to sample everything and to have a weighbridge. We glibly accept whatever we are sent without checking either the quality or the weight. Can you think of anything we sell which isn't either sampled or weighed, probably both? Don't forget we are the only industry I know of where we buy everything at retail and sell everything at wholesale and have no say in either price.

Pigs have always been that bit different and that more special. The industry has been inundated with welfare regulations for not only animals but humans also. Nothing wrong with that you might think and I would go along with that. It makes it all the more galling therefore when the industry has had legislation thrust upon it, which has cost approaching £300 million for the removal of and the replacement for sow stalls, plus the banning of meat and bone meal, because as the retailers have said, that is what their customers want, then they nip off and buy foreign pig meat because it is so much cheaper. But it is never explained to their customers that they are not being offered the safest product in the world. Our competitors have not had to spend on welfare and they have had the advantage of feeding meat and bone meal, probably £4 per pig. So, how can any government allow meat to come into this country, which is obviously of inferior standard, produced in inferior conditions? The standard reply is that to prevent it would be a distortion of free trade. Was it not then distortion of free trade when the EU banned British beef because of an assumed risk? Nor is it distortion of free trade when the French who are much more nationalistic than us, set fire to lorries containing English lamb, if imports distort their own trade, or when they tip over lorries containing Spanish vegetables?

So then the price of pigs collapsed and it took that down-turn for our pig industry to unite as one to lobby the retailers to honour requests for welfare friendly, safe, top quality products. I must say those demonstrations were highly successful and had a tremendous effect on what appeared on the super-market shelves, so we now know our responsibility does not stop at the farm gate, more likely it starts there. Maybe we were becoming a bit more like the French at that time and just that little bit more militant. I know the police were keeping a dos-sier on the marches and demonstrations, but so far as I know, no one ever stepped out of line. We took the decision that it was not necessary and would only alienate us from our retail-ers and perhaps even the public. As it was the public were very supportive, and as we had thought, they really did not have any idea of what was happening or even what they were being offered. So much for the customers having told the retailers what they wanted! Nevertheless, I still believe the customers vote with their purses. They have a set amount to spend and generally source the cheapest possible. On my travels abroad,

I have visited countries that do supply us with pig meat. Some farms are probably up to our standards but there are a hell of a lot which are not. Again it was galling to find out that some of our retailers had accepted this situation and even given extra time to comply, whilst crucifying us here if we had not.

Pigs have always been cyclical but the 1998 recession was by far and away the worst on record and it lasted for six years! We had a series of events all coinciding, which included our high interest rates and strong Sterling, and the collapse of the Russian market at the same time as the financial mess in the Far East, two major importers of our pig meat. There have been massive increases in pig meat production in Europe and the United States, but not here in Britain as we are one of very few European countries not to be self-sufficient. Pig meat can be produced cheaply in the United States and Canada, where feed is probably half of our price. Our only saving grace is to persuade our retailers to forego a bit of profit and to pay us for what they asked for, a sufficient price to keep our lads in business. I suppose we are crackers really, it takes us ten months to produce a pig, we are told what we are going to get for it, the supermarkets sell it within a week and make more than we do, and do not pay for it until it has been sold. It must be a rather nice way to make money.

I have always been a believer in education but the best education you can get is in the University of Life. Just study people and they will tell you all you want to know. Life is one long experience and we never stop learning. Oh, I know we have to learn to read and write and how to add up. If possible we have to learn another language or two, learn about finance, computers and all the modern carrying-on we have, but give me a practical guy every time. When I went to Askham Bryan, there were very few agricultural colleges in the country. Over the years, they have mushroomed as farming developed. Now, as farming numbers are in decline and less and less men are wanted on farms, even the colleges are feeling the draught a bit, they are having to become self-financing and offer other subjects. Small animals and horses are favourites, countryside pursuits, game-keeping, landscape gardening, and all sorts of other courses just to keep going, and most of them becoming part of a university. Many colleges ran pig courses, which were a great success. Now you will be hard pressed to find a full time course. There is much more emphasis on farm training, probably to save time and from a disease point of view. Years ago we freely visited each other's farms and walked around the pigs, in fact we were proud to show them off. There was no such thing as showering in or out, and we never even cleaned our boots and I have yet to find what disease we took round with us, none I suspect, but in the name of progress, we now have quicker growing pigs which are probably like their own-ers, more susceptible to stress therefore to disease also. One thing I hate doing is showering on farms before entering a unit. I reckon that if I showered at home and I was pig free, there is no reason on earth to do it again. I will probably be shot down now by the vets!

Pig World is now coming up to its twentieth anniversary. I suppose by now, I know most of the people in the companies associated with our industry. That in itself is a bonus, to meet the men and women who make these companies tick. Thank goodness the Government can't tax me on that, as they try on everything else! I have always felt that it was our duty on *Pig World* to bring to pig farmers, whatever might be of interest to them and if we only help a couple of chaps with each issue, then surely it has all been worthwhile. I am not by any stretch of the imagination a salesman. However, when *Pig World* first started

I was given the responsibility for everything connected with it, including generating revenue. After all, it is the revenue that buys the editorial space. That has been one hell of a learning curve. At first companies were very sceptical about what was seen as a regional rag and this humble country peasant who stumbled and fumbled his way round. Gradually it dawned on them that perhaps we were here to stay and yes, we did get one or two useful pieces of information published. Selling advertising must be the most soul-destroying job on earth. So many want early right hand pages, and of course they want it for next to nowt, a bit like farmers really! I suppose being a farmer first and foremost does give me an advantage when some advertising agencies need information about pigs. I have often been sent items to try and I have always been honest enough to give an opinion. Several times I have turned away advertising because I felt the product was not good enough. Perhaps that has stood me in good stead, never take money under false pretences.

So what else has *Pig World* done for me? It has enabled me to build on that confidence first gained in the Young Farmers movement. I am delighted to have been asked to chair many meetings and conferences for a host of different firms. I have had the pleasure of addressing discussion groups up and down the country and to have given after dinner talks to all sorts of organisations. Perhaps what gave me the greatest satisfaction of all was when I was asked to do the honours at my former Young Farmers Club when they had their fiftieth and sixtieth anniversaries. I couldn't get over how young they all looked and the girls seemed so much more attractive and were dressed (or perhaps undressed) to kill. The only good thing about reaching the more mature years is the fact that women of a wider age range appeal now!

I had travelled a lot before I started *Pig World*, but since then I have visited every county in the country many times and have contacts in every one. The only difference between then and now is the amount of traffic on the roads and the appalling standard of driving. Company cars were few and far between in my youth, so you grew up respecting vehicles, as you had to pay for them. It is easy to spot the sales representatives in their cars, they just have to go that bit faster, and drive that bit closer, usually with a mobile phone glued to their ear and their jacket hanging up at a window. If they are always in such a hurry, why on earth don't they set off a bit earlier? That is another great advancement, mobile phones. Whatever did we do without them? Well I will tell you, we had a much more peaceful life and we still got by perhaps because the pace of life was much slower.

People ask me if I ever dry up for subjects to write about? The answer is that it has not happened so far and the biggest problem has always been each month, not what we put in but what we leave out. The other question is do I ever get sick of travelling the length and breadth of the country and with driving itself? The answer is no. There is always something new to see, and fresh faces to meet and I really enjoy my driving. I developed at an early age, a 'feel' for a vehicle, as though it were a live thing and had a soul and I try to feel as one with whatever I am driving. I have driven well over a million miles and only ever had three breakdowns and one accident when some dubious looking people ran through red lights and caused £5,000 of damage. Once I had a fan belt break, a fuel pump pack up and also a cylinder head gasket. Other than those three times, I have always arrived home again safe and sound. One thing I have always insisted on be it car, tractor or lawn mower and that is never to miss a service – never. I can't abide to see vehicles which are obviously neglected, dints in them, wheel hub caps missing, lights out, you know the sort of thing and if I hear someone trying to start a car and it misfires due to lack of maintenance, I really get quite uptight. Cars that are not serviced are a menace and a danger on the road. Very often in accidents, it is not what you do but someone else's mistake.

14 | Australasia

sia and Australia have always fascinated me but apart from my trip to Korea and Hong Kong in 1989, I had never had the opportunity to go. The new millennium saw all that change with an invitation from JSR Healthbred Pigs to visit Thailand, Philippines and Australia with a view to looking at their very successful breeding operations. Brian Edwards, the Managing Director visits the Far East four times a year so is well-versed in protocol and procedures, an extremely important aspect of life, particularly in Asia. The Australians are, well how shall I put it, a breed of their own, very laid back and some could almost be called brash. I don't mean this in any offensive way, it is their way of displaying confidence and they all have plenty of that. They are fortunate to live in a young country, a developing country, and without doubt one which is going places. A population of around 20 million for a country almost the size of America gives some indication.

Humberside Airport was the beginning of the journey, via Amsterdam, then on to Kuala Lumpur and from there, to Manila, the capital of that fascinating country, the Philippines. I say country, difficult one really as it is made up of 700 islands - at low tide! Unfortunately, there is much strife and political unrest there, particularly in the south. Apart from security guards and the odd civilian carrying guns, we did not experience any of the unrest but the guns are a constant reminder and I was amused one day at a restaurant where there was a basket for any gun carriers to deposit their weapon whilst they ate!

Something strikes you when you first visit a foreign country and in Manila it was the humidity and the enormous traffic jams, which obviously mean a lot of pollution. Street vendors, policemen, those sweeping the streets, all wore face masks be-

Traffic in Manilla!

cause of the fumes. Buses had no windows, a sort of basic air conditioning I suppose which is very much needed. I compare the traffic there with that of Bangkok, two cities of similar size with similar population density and I honestly can't decide which is worst, they are both appalling. Bangkok has proper cars and the famous Tuk tuks – a three-wheeler motorcycle type of machines – whilst in Manila, the Jeepneys reign supreme. These are modelled on long wheel based Jeeps which have had a variety of bodies built onto them. Most have bench seats running the full length, plus steps at the back and grab rails on the side, as often passengers cling on and they are nearly always overloaded. I think the policemen directing traffic must take their lives in their hands every day.

We know that Asia is by-and-large poor or at least the vast majority of people are. There is also wealth in the Philippines and the difference between opulence and abject poverty can be cut by a knife it is so plain to see. However, poverty does not deter the people from being courteous and extremely helpful.

A 'Jeepney'.

They have a different culture from us, maybe to do with Buddhism but they could not have been kinder or more welcoming. Rice is without doubt the staple diet of the whole of Asia, grown each year on the same paddy, apparently fairly disease free to boot.

What I found throughout Asia, and in that I include the Philippines, Thailand, China and Vietnam, is that the poorer people are happy with what they do not have and I often think there is a salutary lesson for us who live in a more prosperous society. They make all kinds of things from virtually nothing that they are happy to sell you on the roadside or the streets in town. They will grow a few vegetables or perhaps fruit and sell those too for a few pence. I believe that paid labour is remunerated at around £4.50 per working day in the Philippines which is £2 more than Thailand, in Vietnam £1 per day and in China about fifty pence with its 1.2 billion population.

Driving out to the farm near Manila which took around three hours, the whole way virtually had tin shacks at the side of the road with flea bitten dogs and children in rags but every-body seemed happy, and they all wave, but it was also notice-able that each shack had a colour television.

Arriving at the farm there was not only security but very strict bio-security for the 1,500 sow multiplication unit, which incidentally did have a high wall all the way around and the former gun turrets were still in evidence. I enquired as to why and was told it was to stop the locals rustling the pigs! The whole of the car including the roof was disinfected as it drove through the wheel dip and two men, with what looked like small pressure washers, actually did a thorough job with the disinfectant. Could this be an area, that is neglected in Britain? The entrance to the farm which is shut when nothing is passing through is actually manned around the clock.

The unit was huge and fairly well spread out and it was the first time I had ever seen specialist pig buildings without any walls. They had overhanging eaves to keep the sun and the rain away from the pigs and the pens, which actually formed

Typical Philippine piggery.

the edge of the buildings. There were four female vets working there and I lost count of the number of actual workers, but the pigs looked superb and obviously the management input from Brian Edwards, who also holds the role of Chairman of the Australian JSR Hyfarms, which supply breeding stock to Asia, was beginning to have effect. All the staff gathered round to listen about the rudiments of pig keeping, even for things like clipping teeth and tails, the right way to inject, and on a higher level, the use and practice of AI from their own station complete with laboratory. One thing I did see Brian pick up on, and I suppose it would not be the first farm for it to happen, was in the AI laboratory; they had disposable equipment for many items but to try and save money some members of staff were washing the equipment. Once it was explained why they should not do this they accepted it readily.

The Samientos family who owned the pig farm also owned a large feed mill and supplement business in Manila but as yet there are no bulk feed facilities on farms so all feed came in bags and dozens of men would appear to unload the lorries. A

Sam with the staff of Philippines' pig farm.

fascinating visit, the memories of which remain with me to this day, as do the rest of my Asian jaunts which since then have been numerous. Even now three of the girl vets keep in touch although none of them are still employed at the farm. One is a lecturer, and the other two are employed by animal health companies.

The next leg of the journey was with Quantas from Manila to Sydney and although I have not spent time in Sydney, the Harbour Bridge and Opera House are very impressive when viewed from the air and I am sure are equally so at ground level. A change of plane for the flight to Brisbane, which either from the air, and maybe more so from the ground, is more than impressive. It is amazing how it has developed in 150 years. It is very beautiful with 1100 parks and masses of wide, open, green spaces. I have a nephew living there so was able to spend the weekend with him. He has an enviable life style, superb climate, surfing, diving, swimming, has a new four wheel drive and has built his own house, and of course there is plenty of good 'tucker' as they call food in Australia. He and I had a meal one evening at a beautiful restaurant on the side of the river, having arrived there on a super fast boat. We both had sizeable steaks with all the trimmings and a bottle of wine, total cost £14.00! His young daughter has a superb environment in which to grow up and Adam does not see any reason for coming back to Britain other than to see family.

The Hyfarm headquarters is at Toowoomba about 100 miles west from Brisbane and is known as Garden City and is certainly well named. Hyfarm at that time had two nucleus units, both north from Toowoomba, one we visited by car, a bit of a drive and the other by plane. Queensland is vast with about every kind of farming and environment that you could wish for. Water is, I believe, the limiting factor in further development.

There are only about 300,000 sows in Australia and 20,000,000 people. Ten percent of both are in Western Australia, which I visited two years later. That means that pigs are kept far apart, one reason why the health level is so high and another is because of the strict bio-security. One other reason is that they do not allow livestock into the country and if any semen is allowed in, it has to be whiter than white and it is extremely difficult to obtain a licence. JSR managed to get some in through their Norwegian genetic pool where disease is practically non-existent. When we landed at Sydney the Customs officer, once he knew we were involved in farming, told us we had Foot and Mouth in Britain, which we did not know about but he was

Gilts for sale in the Philippines

right, so he made us take off our shoes and remove any others from our bag for disinfection. Of course he was right so to do and our Government could well take a lesson or two from this practice. Incidentally, at that time there were 84 sniffer dogs at airports in Australia and how many did we have - none! That altered in 2002, we obtained two dogs, which doubled to four by 2004. Doesn't that tell you everything? Having said that the Customs were given the job of checking for illegal meat coming into Britain, they didn't catch much the first year but were given extra resources the second and by the end of 1993, they had seized tonnes and tonnes of things like rats and monkey meat. These are apparently considered as delicacies by certain ethnic minorities in London. It is a dangerous practice to bring in illegal meat, and indeed some legal meat, as standards of health and hygiene are not always as high as we have in this country, and of the half-dozen diseases we had here in the late 1990s and early in the new millennium, none of them were indigenous, so had to have come from imported sources.

The Australian pig farms are well dispersed as land is plentiful and for nothing. Again they have open-sided buildings but with a curtain system to be drawn at night in winter as nights can be cold. Apart from that and the fact the sows are washed every day and all piggeries washed down, you could imagine you were in a British piggery. The slurry and the washing water go into lagoons away from the farm and simply evaporate, or if there is an arable farmer near he might come and take the slurry away. Stalls are still the ideal way to keep sows and I guess anywhere as far as that goes as it does allow for individual management. Australia has a high priced export of 'green' pork to Asia, Singapore, Hong Kong and Japan in particular. They are close enough for fresh pork to be flown to these destinations without the need for freezing. I could have spent a week there without any problem as there was so much to see, Maize, rice, bananas, sugar cane, cereals, a host of vegetables, and of course cattle. A young expanding thriving country with a laid back attitude to most things except we Poms but at least they helped us in both wars.

Flying from Brisbane we landed at Melbourne and then an eight hour flight to Bangkok. I think almost four hours of that was over the centre of Australia, which seemed endless ranges of hills and dry unexplored valleys and plains. If the plane had come down they never would have found us.

In Thailand I was introduced to Dr Suchat Prommano who has subsequently become a good friend and is a pig and dairy adviser on nutrition and veterinary matters. He always arranges visits for me when I go back and I have been back sixteen times. I like Thailand very much, the people are so friendly and helpful and they have a superb culture that includes looking after Granny instead of putting her in a home. The Thai pig industry is twice the size of ours, and as more and more British genetics find their way there, the performance and the

Australian pig-breeding unit, J.S.R. Nucleus Unit.

Open-sided quarantine sector, Thailand unit.

carcase quality of their pigs have almost doubled. They do eat most of the product but have one state-of-the-art export abattoir as good as anything we have. This is with a view to supplying Singapore, Hong Kong and Japan in competition with Australia. Open sided piggeries again, something I always find unusual but it works and works well. That obviously cheapens the cost of building. There is about 20% of the production in what I would call good modern units with performances to almost match that in Britain. The other 80% like Vietnam and China is still kept in backyard or small family units. They are very labour intensive but this does not seem to matter, as there is plenty of cheap labour. Away from farming, which in itself is very diverse as Thailand is the same size as France, there is plenty for tourists to do and see. Travel north to Chiang-rai or Chiang-mai and you can go elephant trekking. This is an awesome experience. These magnificent beasts are so strong yet so gentle and place their huge feet very carefully with each step. Travel south to Phuket which is a favourite holiday resort and there are trips available to many different islands, one of which is the famous James Bond island shot in the film *The Man With The Golden Gun*. All the usual seaside activities are available including riding a banana boat, paragliding, jet skiing and of course swimming in beautiful, clear, blue water. The food is out of this world with an array of fruit and vegetables we never see here. It is also incredibly cheap. I remember having a very nice hotel in the north at Lampang for five nights with break-fast and the total bill was £41.50.

There is a superb agricultural show every two years in Bangkok for the whole of Asia which I now go to, it keeps you in touch with what is happening, and believe me it is happen-ing. Asia is bubbling and will soon be an economy to be en-vied, the same with China and probably more so. Recently, a conference on livestock production for Asia, again held in the superb facilities of the Queen Sirikit Exhibition Centre, which was attended by delegates from all over the world and five of the speakers were from Britain, such is the esteem in which we are held. I have been to many farms many times and can't fail to notice the expansion. When the dreaded Asian avian 'flu struck their poultry industry it was devastating, similar to how it was here when Foot and Mouth struck. It had the immediate effect of putting up the price of their pork and for the first time in a long time pig producers made money. It devastated their whole economy, as exporting poultry meat is a massive busi-ness. In fact the whole of Asia exists by exporting the produce of their cheap labour, which is why you now find call centres in Mumbai and your shirts made in Taiwan. All manner of crops are grown but rice has to be the mainstay. The people live on rice and stir-fry every day for about thirty pence. They do ex-port rice and coffee and if you watch the traffic on the river run-ning through Bangkok, you will see the tug boats hauling massive barges on their way to the docks with produce for export. I like Thailand so much I could retire there quite easily. The language is a bit of a difficulty with 44 letters in their alphabet, none of them anything like any of ours although I don't think it would be as difficult to learn as Chinese or Japanese.

I had an abortive trip to China in 1992. I had been to Hong Kong years before but never to mainland China. The VIV Beijing agricultural show was the reason for going. I made all the travel arrangements or so I thought. I arrived at Beijing airport heeding the warning of the plane crew to be aware of illegal taxis. They will try to rip you off they said so fix a price first. The proper price was apparently 100 Yuen. The first chop approached me and he wanted 250. Eventually I got one for 120 Yuen but unfortunately the hotel had changed its name since I had booked it so that was a bit of fun as the driver did not speak English.

The show itself was like any other show in layout but to see all the foreign names there made you realise just how vulnerable you were if you got lost. I had two contacts who had arranged visits for me, one about an hour from Beijing and when it came to the time to depart for the visit, we received a phone call to say we could not go. I asked why and my contact, an Australian, said no reason had to be given, we simply could not go! The second visit was two-and-a-half hours away by plane to a place called Chongqing that apparently is the largest or the most densely populated city in China with 30 million people. It also has one of the most densely populated pig areas. At the airport I was duly met by a driver and interpreter who looked after me very well that weekend when I visited several of the tourist areas. Come Monday morning we arrived at an extremely modern piggery where I was told I could not look around as I was there on the wrong day, I should come back in two days. It wasn't the wrong day and in two days I would be on my way back home. So all I finished up seeing there were some backyard pigs kept in appalling conditions and an abattoir which was even worse. Five men would lift the large fat pigs onto a wooden thrawl, tie their feet and then cut their throats. The de-hairing and removal of guts took place in the same area, something that would not be tolerated here. Rats were running around and there was a heap of coal for firing the hot water, again all in the same area. Apparently most of the backyard pigs are dealt with in this manner and I couldn't get away fast enough. Thus, I left China with not too good an impression. I will return one day when hopefully appointments will be kept. There are of course some very good modern farms, both livestock and arable in China, but the peasant farming I believe will ever be so because of the small hillside plots available, where they are either worked by hand or oxen. Modern machinery would not be able to function.

Flying back over Mongolia and then Siberia made me realise how lucky we are to be in Britain despite the Government, rules, regulations and taxes.

15 | Worries

mentioned previously about driving and the land I rented at Leconfield, the former RAF base. The actual camp
is presently occupied by the Air Sea Rescue helicopter
squadron and home to the Army Driving School. They also
train Navy and Air Force drivers. That means there are over
800 vehicles ranging from minis to heavy lifting gear trucks
and snow cats running about on our local roads. None of them
ever exceed 40 mph and quite frequently cause traffic jams.
I suppose we have learned to live with them. Each year the
Brigadier invites various locals to a ceremony called 'Beating
Retreat'. I suppose I qualified as a tenant of the land there.
I remember once saying to one of the former Brigadiers that
his trucks were a bloody nuisance and what was he going to
do about it? He looked at me and asked me whether I would
rather follow the lorries or look down the barrel of an enemy
tank? There are no foreign tanks I replied, to which he said,
well just think how effective we are!

I have also had the opportunity of driving some of the vehicles
and I can assure you it is great fun driving a snow cat. Because
of my experience with tractors, I coped very well, which rather
surprised the instructor, as apparently they are not the easiest
things to reverse.

I have often thought about what the Brigadier said, I took
his point and yes the lads do get a thorough training which will
stand them in good stead in case of action. The basic course is
six weeks with another six for the heavy stuff. It has to be said
that the base generates a lot of local trade, particularly in the
pubs in Beverley on a Saturday night!

When I was growing vegetables on the land at Leconfield,
I used to call on them to provide fork lift trucks for loading the
boxes onto lorries. That helped me, and also helped them as

it provided the men with a real job instead of moving empty crates around all the time. Of course we had to abide by certain rules and regulations and give way to traffic signs. I remember one occasion before straw burning was banned we had started a right good blaze but had forgotten to mention it to the commanding officer. All hell let loose and the station fire engines appeared en masse! Fortunately, they allowed us to finish what we were doing and they actually stayed behind to mind the dying embers, again perhaps a useful exercise for them.

I know I wrote in an earlier chapter that this land had been taken back for tree-planting purposes – it was, but only part of it, and since relented on the remainder until harvest in 2002. I recall when the station closed as an RAF base to become Humberside Airport for a couple of years before moving to Kirmington. It was extremely handy for popping down to London.

The runways had obviously been well illuminated and the land I farmed runs up to the edge of some of the minor runways. I decided some years ago that we would subsoil the whole lot, as I was sure it was a bit tough down under. We did and we gathered up quite a collection of cables. Fortunately, all the power had been disconnected, or if it hadn't it certainly would have been after that little exercise!

So having gone full circle, that is starting off by using a contractor, doing the work ourselves, and having livestock enterprises, where do I go from here? What will happen to farming and the countryside? What will happen to England as a country? Will our beloved Government knacker up all industries as successfully as they have agriculture and some of its associated industries? Will we be able to compete in the export markets with our Sterling still strong and relatively high interest rates? How much more can we produce on farms? Perhaps the question is how much more do the Government want us to produce? Currently everything is a bad trade including potatoes and milk, and sugar beet C quota means many acres will be disced in. There is supposedly too much food globally, yet still half the population is hungry, whilst the only hunger the other half has is its greed. What is the future of family farming? I wish I knew the answers.

If you were to farm in Italy, Greece, France or Spain for example, the answer could well be different. Why is it we British abide by rules and regulations? If a stupid law comes out of Brussels on a Friday at five in the afternoon, our civil servants in Whitehall would sit around a table at ten-thirty the following Monday, having had a coffee first, to see how they could enforce this law and if all farmers had not complied by that Monday night, how much fine they could impose on them. In any other country, the powers-that-be would be around the table at seven in the morning, having already had breakfast, and wondering how they could assist the farmers to avoid having to comply. Perhaps this is a bit of poetic licence, but it has more than a smattering of truth in it. Some of the EU member countries appear to disobey rules, such as milk quotas, acreage payments, giving help to pig farmers, so many things. Perhaps it is their Latin temperaments, or does the trouble lie with our stiff upper lip and determination?

I do worry about new blood coming into the industry, where are the opportunities? Pigs and poultry used to be the only way in, but now that entry is barred. How do we encourage people to farm when we are the butt of all jokes yet still seen as landed gentry who produce far too much food and receive huge subsidies for the privilege. The paltry amounts paid out in subsidies is a portion of what the supermarkets take out of us every year, but no one seems to mind, least of all the customers who perceive them as being convenient. Each year there are less and less people around who remember ration books. Perhaps the public are too well fed, they are certainly spoiled for choice and of course it is agriculture which has given them choice. Perhaps more people should heed the notice seen recently on the side of a lorry, 'Don't knock farmers with your mouth full'.

What many fail to realise is that the majority of farmers have borrowings because of the nature of the business. If we make a profit, we get landed with a tax bill, which as far as I am concerned is a waste of money. If you don't make a profit and there is little of that about currently, then the banks are not pleased. A paper profit might reduce your borrowings on paper but when the tax bill comes, the money is not there, as the borrowings have soared again following two disastrous harvests, which have gobbled up any prior savings made. What a weird world we live in.

The immediate problem for all of us is the immediate future. The long-term future is for another day, yet we ought to be making preparations for it now, but many farmers don't have the money to lay the plans. What was once an average size farm, like mine (200 acres) or so, when I came here 30 years ago, is now a small farm and never likely to be let again as a unit. Will it in due course revert to the landlord only to be swallowed up by a large conglomerate, farmed under a management programme, or will it go to one or several of my neighbour's sons? I don't know the answer to that and I don't really want to find out yet - the tenancy is my pension! So long as I am able to walk the farm, coordinate operations and don't have to do any of the work myself, I see no reason why I shouldn't carry on until I am 75.

The farming cycles we are seeing now are becoming more

frequent and more serious. The 1997 and 1998 harvests must surely go down as some of the worst this century. The BSE crisis decimated the beef industry, the dairy boys are taking a hammering on the price of milk, yet it keeps on going up on the doorstep. Pigs have been an absolute disaster but showed a recovery in 2003. I had a gut feeling that the 2003 harvest would be better both physically and financially. I was wrong again. It will not take much of a lift in prices to get us back to profitability and provided yields are at the levels we have grown accustomed to, that will be an added bonus. The downturn has caused casualties and there are bound to be more. Doubtless we will see a shakeout in the pig sector. I don't care how rich you are, losses of up to £30 per pig are unsustainable for long periods.

Abattoirs are becoming larger and fewer, so outlets are reduced. Retailers are becoming even larger and even greedier and they control our destiny. I look forward to the day when we have a partnership with retailers, with our produce being geared to the retail price, so we all have an equal share of the proceeds.

Perhaps our milling wheats should be related to bread prices as bread prices despite protestation from the bakers bear no relation to the price of milling wheat, and similarly our malting barleys to beer prices. Perhaps our livestock prices should be related in some way also to feed costs or the retail price. We do not live in an ideal world, but there must be a more realistic one out there somewhere. We can't all be plc-orientated, or, should we have Great Britain plc? It strikes me today that our big companies are just money-driven without any human compassion. Farmers have always been compassionate to people and animals alike. They have always been successful business men, without until recently having to be business men and I don't say that lightly. Do your job right in the past and the end result was such as you could live comfortably, maintain hedges, ditches and buildings, replace equipment when necessary, refurbish buildings as they needed it, and even keep pace with modern technology. Now we have targets and a drive to make men redundant in the name of efficiency. It is a numbers game, making figures fit, slashing costs sometimes beyond what is necessary.

It would be interesting to come back in a hundred years to see if the land is still farmed in the same way, or whether the populous is living on pills made by robots in a sterile factory, whilst farms are all national parks. Will newspapers still exist? Will magazines like *Pig World* (well, there are none quite like *Pig World*) still be published? Maybe every house will have a personal computer and access to the internet, or will that have become outmoded? If advertising is still used will that appear on the screens instead of in print? I am sure there will be many changes, which makes me wonder how much use we should be making of the internet now.

If changes do take place as I am sure they will, how will people spend their extended leisure time? Will there be even more crime and drug abuse? What will we do when petrol is no longer available? There are so many, many things on which to ponder.

One thing I do know is that I am proud to be a farmer, to have been part of a developing industry, and indeed, I still hope to be a part of the future for some considerable time yet. After all, banging away on a typewriter, sorry, I mean a word processor, doesn't take a lot of effort and having just spent a fortune on two new pairs of spectacles, I can still see the screen very clearly. I just wish I could see the way ahead as clearly but it is like driving through fog and the new CAP single payment scheme has caused more headaches than it has cured. All farmers want to do, and are good at, is to farm and produce what they were trained to do, good quality, safe, nourishing food for the nation.

16 Distant Memories

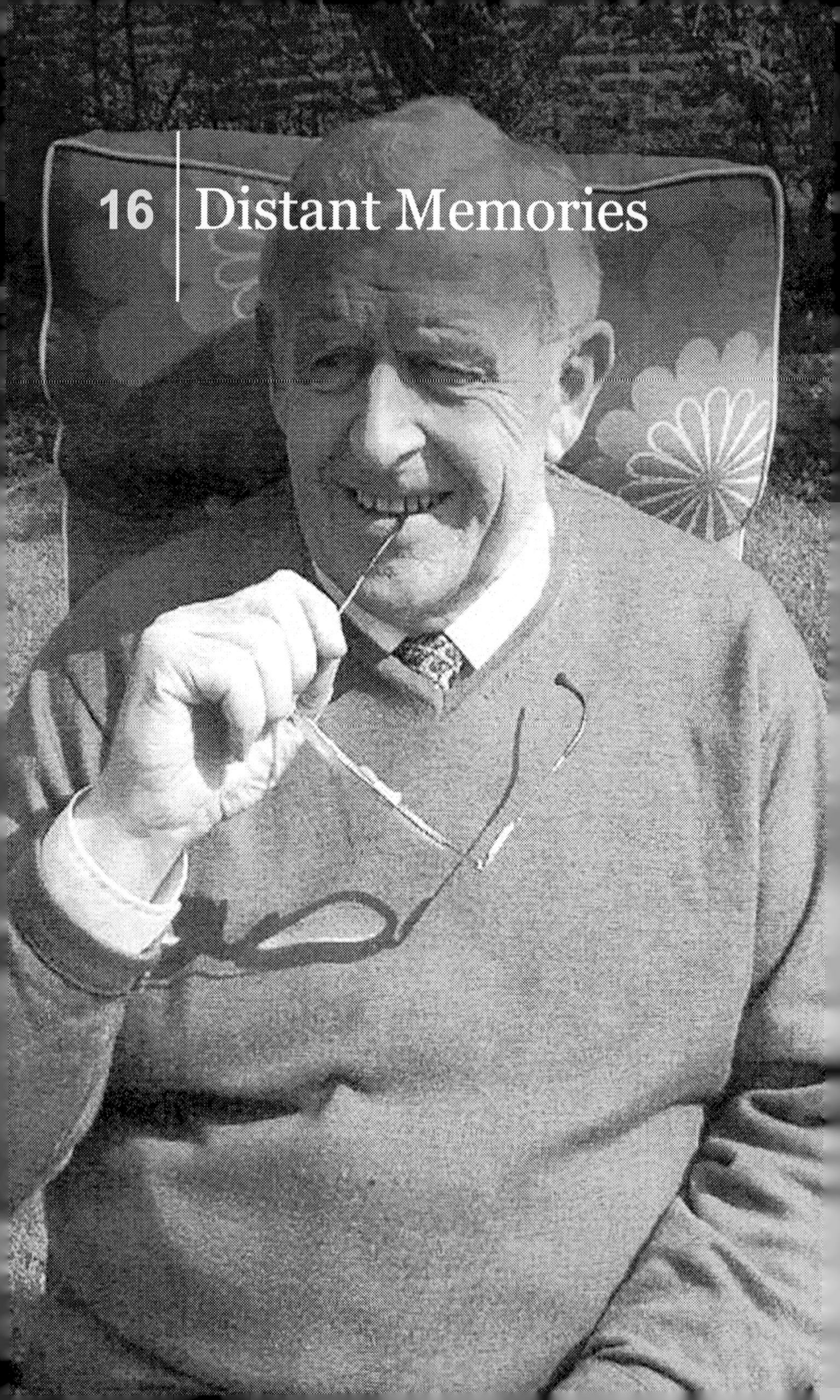

Of course it isn't just agriculture which is suffering from cheap imports. Our clothing industry has been decimated in favour of countries like Cyprus, India, and further over into Asia and latterly China. Coal mining was a massive industry for decades and look what happened to that. Today, we have tonnes of imported coal from Eastern Europe and Australia fulfilling all our needs or most of them. How on earth does it make economic sense to import coal from Australia? The ship that transports it will use thousands of gallons of fossil fuel and all that achieves is to use up reserves for nothing and to blow a larger hole in the ozone layer. What utter madness. The son of a friend of mine occasionally helps out a haulier. He spent all one week collecting imported coal from Poland, delivering it to stockpiles on former colliery sites and on the way back went to a quarry to pick up stone to tip down a local mine shaft so it couldn't easily be opened again. Is it any wonder the miners are bitter?

The more I travel the more I see what our Government obviously cannot, that other countries have support in various guises from their own political rulers. Farming is a basic commodity and the oldest profession (bar one!) and all we are doing is allowing our jobs to be exported and contribute to the ruination of the rural economy.

Several years ago, the Government of Western Australia gave several presentations in a bid to recruit young families to immigrate and they were offered opportunities to start up in farming or take responsible positions on someone else's farm. The presentations were highly successful and I know personally several families who took up the offer. Other countries appreciate the quality of our workers and businessmen. I decided to go to Australia to see for myself.

Perth in Western Australia is the most isolated city in the world. Have a look at an atlas you will see what I mean. It is also one of the most beautiful with the magnificent Swan River running through and it is an experience to travel by boat from Freemantle up to Perth. Not unlike the former Salisbury and Bulawayo in Zimbabwe in layout, inasmuch as the streets run one way and the avenues the other, so you can't really get lost. The climate is superb, does not get above 40 °C or below 3°C. The cost of living is half that of here while the wages are pretty similar. It is a developing part of Australia and the Government is doing its best to encourage entrepreneurial skills. Their agricultural advisory service is superb and extremely support-ive. They will help you locate a site for a business or find suit-able land to farm. They are supporting export drives to Asia for a number of agricultural products, and new abattoirs and processing factories are being built. There is very little red tape and the families who have immigrated absolutely love it, and it is a great place for kids to grow up. I was extremely impressed with what I saw and the hospitality was superb. Here in Brit-ain it seems as if every possible obstacle is put in the way of progress and parents are now paranoid about child safety.

*   *   *

Until 2004, I had never actually set foot in Canada. I had seen it across the Niagara Falls and had thought what a magnificent city Toronto appeared to be. I was invited to an International Conference on Probiotics in Montreal so thought why not? Something like 80% of the Canadian population lives within 100 kilometres of the American border so that is where the ma-jority of the production and the good farming are. On this occa-sion I did not have to travel to Heathrow, I flew from Humber-side. First stop was Amsterdam, a change of plane and direct to

Montreal. The plane had been delayed getting to Humberside from Amsterdam so we were an hour late arriving across the Channel. That only left me twenty-five minutes to get across Schipol airport, and the boarding gates were about to close as I arrived panting in the nick of time. I did wonder if that was a bad omen as very often I have incidents on my travels like suitcases going astray, missing connections and so many unanticipated things. When I arrived in Montreal my suitcase was a long time in appearing and I was about to give up on it when it appeared last of all. I thought no more of it and it was not until the next morning when I wanted my camera that I realised it had been taken from my suitcase. The camera case was still there though, very clever that, take the camera, leave its case; it fooled me for twelve hours or so.

I reported it to hotel security and they duly checked the CCT tapes. No one but me had entered my room since I arrived so that meant it had to have happened in Humberside, Schipol or Montreal. I also went to the police station but they obviously couldn't do anything other than give me a crime number for the insurance. It was a brand new expensive digital and the next day being Sunday none of the department stores were open - they are still civilised there - so I couldn't buy another one. That was a great pity as I spent three hours on a coach going around Montreal and there were plenty of photographic opportunities. The next day was the full day Conference with photographs supplied of the speakers and on the Tuesday morning when we all toured the world's largest yeast producing plant, we were not allowed to take shots anyway, so I solved the problem of no camera that day also. The Tuesday afternoon I was flying to Toronto so I thought never mind I will buy another camera in Montreal airport. Not one to be seen anywhere! A great pity because it was a clear day and the farms seemed to go on forever, really beautiful countryside. I decided I would buy a camera in Toronto airport. Not a chance, none there either!

I needed to be at a town called Stratford about 120 miles or so from Toronto and when I landed I had no idea how I was going to get there. Would there be a coach, a train or would I need to hire a car? The first information cubicle I came to the lady was very helpful inasmuch as she took the bookings for a mini-coach, which actually did the Stratford run, and I was dropped at my hotel door and collected again two days later, most efficient. I thought I would buy a camera in the town there but they don't seem to have cameras shops like we do here.

The reason I wanted to go to Stratford was to attend the Canadian National Pig Fair, and it seemed such a shame not to do that when I was only a couple of hours or so away. Of course I was worried about not being able to take photographs whilst at the Fair but I need not have worried, a friend was launching his pig product Gleptosil iron for piglets at the Fair, and he kindly loaned me his camera for the day.

When I got back to Schipol I went to the airport police who thanked me for informing them about the theft of my camera and that they knew something was going on and had installed surveillance cameras. Of course it never turned up so the moral of the story is don't put anything of value in your suitcase, carry it with you. When I contacted the National Farmers Union Insurance Company about the loss, the girl who took my details said that she too had clothes taken from her suitcase coming back from Spain.

At the Pig Fair I met three people whom I knew when they were working in Britain, all had emigrated and none would return. It is a similar situation to Western Australia, but much colder in the winter. Even that they say in the mid-Canadian

States is not a problem, and that is where the bulk of pig production is concentrated. Temperatures get down as low as minus 50 ^{0}C now and then, but they have more sunshine than California. One problem they do have if the temperature plummets to around minus 50 is that they cannot transport pigs as they will freeze to the side of the lorries and of course if that happens, they tear great chunks of flesh off! Water pipes are buried below a metre deep and buildings are insulated way beyond anything we would need to do. That means they must get their ventilation right.

The standard of living in Canada is much higher, the cost much lower, how about petrol at thirty-five pence per litre and that was after a 10% lift in price! There is plenty of space in Canada so nowhere seems crowded. Houses all have lots of lawn and garden. Taxi fares in Stratford were a straight six bucks wherever you wanted to go in town. The restaurants were plentiful and excellent, I had never eaten bison before! They also had some unusual names their restaurants - one was called 'Wok and Roll'.

What really impressed me was the help the farmers were given to produce their pig meat. They are still allowed to keep sows in stalls, we cannot. They can still bury dead pigs, we cannot. They have meaningful contracts with retailers on a cost plus basis although Walmart had moved into Canada and they were becoming anxious about what effect that might have. Our contracts are pretty meaningless. Help is given to them to export and they claim to have the best pork in the world. Whether they have or not is not the issue, but even if it were, it would be illegal to produce it in the same way they do if it was in Britain.They are supremely confident in what they do which I guess comes from a hassle-free or almost hassle-free life style.

I could have spent longer there and I was invited back again at some stage for a week to see what Maple Leaf Foods do. They are, shall we say, large integrators. Everything is large there, the tractors, slurry tankers, lorries, cars, you name it, and add to that the size of some of the businesses.

Montreal is very much a French-speaking city built on an island. The St Lawrence Seaway goes as far as Milwalkee and is a tremendous engineering feat. The former Olympic Village is fully occupied now and the stadium with its unique tower is very much a focal point for tourists. Montreal has more trees per head of population than any other city. It is a truly delightful place, as is Toronto on the side of Lake Ontario, which is also the capital of Ontario and is extremely modern. That, thankfully, is English-speaking or at least the sort of English that Canadians speak. One of my friends lives in an apartment overlooking Lake Ontario and he says the view in a morning as the sun rises is breathtaking.

Because of its size, Canadian farmers have economies of scale. The prairies stretch forever and with massive machinery they can cover hundreds of acres in a day. Their hard red milling wheats are world renowned, their beef cattle also and although America is the heaviest subsidised agriculture in the world, they still have to import massive amounts of pig meat from Canada. Good job they do I suppose for the sake of the Canadians.

I said before I could happily retire to Thailand. It would certainly be cheaper than either Western Australia or Canada but I could easily be tempted with either of those too. It is all to do with quality of life. It might appear that I am knocking what we have here. If I am it is not intentional, it is just that visiting so many places an image begins to form in your mind about how other countries are run and what they have to offer. Most places seem to be run for the benefit of the people, which is what I thought the general idea was. Here, I am not sure how important the people are except for paying taxes for the Chancellor to squander! One thing I do know, and it is very, very sad, and that is that farming as we knew it and methods of food production also are gone forever, and we are as a country a lot worse off for it.

One country that I have no desire to return to is Laos the Communist country, which lies to the north east of Thailand. There are not many countries in which I have felt uncomfortable but Laos is certainly one of them but having said that, the ordinary people on family farms are extremely kind and hospitable as well as being extremely poor. There was just something about the aura during my stay that didn't somehow feel right. If I said they lived in fear might be a tad wrong but they are certainly regimented. When you have ten televisions per 1,000 people, eight telephones and three cars, you might begin to get some idea of what things are like. I had hired a minibus in Lampang in the northern part of Thailand for £20 per day plus diesel. It was a nine hour drive through some absolutely stunning mountainous country. I arrived at Nong Khai next to the Laos border and capital city Vientaine. There is a new bridge linking the two countries now and is named the Bridge of Friendship. Thailand drives the same side of the road as we do whereas Laos drives on the right. My minibus was not allowed into Laos, indeed no Thai cars are unless they have permission from the Laos Government. Conversely Laos vehicles can come and go into Thailand pretty much as they please. That meant I had to hire another minibus at the other side, which was twice the price and a wreck to boot. Firstly, though, you have to go through Thai Iimmigration and Customs, board a bus, which takes you over the bridge and then the red tape really starts with the Laos Customs and Immigration. There was a long queue but fortunately, my two guides from Laos who came to see me the previous evening to discuss the programme, knew the ropes and asked me for some Thai baths, about £3, to make an underhand payment to an official. Just as well or I think I would still have been there now.

My good friend and guide in Thailand, Dr Suchat Prommano, seems to know everyone in farming and had a contact in Laos who in turn sent two peasant women to act as guides for me. They had arranged two visits to government run farms. When we arrived at the first one, there a superb office building, but no pigs. They were knocking the buildings down so we asked where the pigs had gone? We duly arrived at the new site but were refused admission, as I had not received official permission. It was unbelievable, and the two women were obviously embarrassed having been assured that everything was in order. So we went for lunch - I had the minibus driver from Laos, the two drivers from Thailand who came with me into Laos, plus the two women guides. The total bill for a nice lunch was 175,000 Kip, which translated to about £8.50! I am not sure if it was the nice lunch which had inspired my guides but they took me to visit two family run pig farms. One woman ran seventeen sows while her husband worked away from the farm, and the next, who seemed to have a large family, had over 100 sows. It was fairly primitive to say the least and I had never before seen weaner accommodation built over water. There were pole barns or sheds that were thatched, they had wire mesh floors and all the droppings and urine went straight into the lakes or ponds to feed the catfish! I was absolutely fascinated as each piglet was carried in and out by hand where the worker walked across a narrow duck board, and all feed was carried in the same way. Similarly, in the finisher accommodation built alongside the lake, the floors were concrete but sloped towards the water. The concrete panelled walls had gaps at the bottom, and each day not only the manure was flushed away into the water but the pigs also got a good washing and literally shone. The larger of the two farms bought feed from neighbouring small farmers in the form of rice, maize and soya beans. They had their own mixing plant which though archaic did the job. The woman, who was very much the boss, always fed the dry and suckling sows and the barrow she used was a tub on runners at waist height. Her sons would carry the feed from the store and fill the barrow up for her. I would say she was a good pig farmer, her results were excellent and the pigs were obviously performing. Trying to find out what the genetics were proved a futile experience, however.

We did a bit of sightseeing; there was much waste land, which is what our farms will grow into soon if we don't come to our senses. Some of the landscape could almost have been classed as jungle. Families tended to bring their native cattle in at nights so often we had to stop the bus to allow the cattle time to get off the dusty pot-holed roads. I was due to have a night in Vientaine but that day had shown me all I was likely to see so by the time I had paid for two minibuses, two guides, bribes, diesel and hotels it was a fairly expensive trip. I understand that the north of Laos is also beautiful, well I will take someone's word for that, I just don't want to know. If that is Communism then you can keep it. The two guides did actually take me to their homes for a few minutes to meet their large families ranging from great-grandmother down to half-a-dozen youngsters, all sitting on the floor. One thing about Asian culture is that they do look after their elders.

Seeing agriculture in that part of the world made me realise how good our land is here, but a problem not particularly unique to Yorkshire is coastal erosion. That is happening at an alarming rate and what do our men in Westminster do? Absolutely nothing! If the Dutch were to inhabit our shores that problem would have been dealt with a century ago and they would also have reclaimed acres of sea. Maybe it is part of our Government's long term plan that at least if the land disappears they will no longer have to worry about it, every acre lost is another acre less on which to produce the food and will give them the opportunity to import even more. The trouble with this attitude is if they keep on letting the land disappear, sooner or later it will reach the point where some of the national park they are trying to provide will also succumb to the elements. Then there will be uproar from the public if their leisure facilities are taken away, but by then it will be too late. We are seeing an increase in population growth, a lot of it from Eastern Europeans who think that Britain is a panacea to their own national difficulties. It may well be but for how long.

My own belief is that we will need every acre of ground we have to be able to come anywhere near self-sufficiency. Surely, as other countries play catch up with us in terms of production costs, which will happen, then there is no possibility that there will be any cheap imported food available. Remember, we may have a global population of over 6 billion people now, but in another fifty years that will rise to 9 billion. China worries me desperately for they will conquer the West financially. In 2000 they had 49 million families of Western standard, reasonable income, ate good food and dressed well. It is expected that by the year 2020, there will be 229 million such families. Where will the food come from? It is a sobering thought but by then I will be but a distant memory!

Good example of a Saddleback.

BRITISH FARMING

Supported By The

SAMARITANS

Robbed By

SUPERMARKETS

T hings have moved on apace since I began to write this epistle several years ago, both in my personal life and that of agriculture. My beloved daughter Romney as soon as she finished University decided she would work in Kuwait as a teacher, which she did for seven years. There she met her future husband, David, a lad from Scotland. We had a lovely wedding in our local church, and those of you who have given away an only daughter will know of the emotions involved; to walk down the aisle and give her away, especially to a Scot! I jest, David is a grand chap and they have presented my wife and I with two beautiful granddaughters, Sophie Grace and Phoebe Eve.

These two are an absolute delight and somehow, although they now live in Abu Dhabi, and I only see them twice a year (when they come for a month in the summer, and when I go out there), I seem to have more time to spend with them than when Romney was their age. Farming has a lot to answer for. Victor on the other hand is still working as an air steward with My Travel visiting exotic places and working with some of the most attractive girls you will ever see. He seems happy enough and his dedicated work has been rewarded as he has been made the company Ambassador, an honour indeed and that was because of his people skills and his exemplary work record. I am pleased for him, as I kept telling him to always do his best and go when called on even if he felt he was being put upon. He has interesting tales to tell about how you see the true British holidaymaker when they have had a drink, and of course what the culture is like in some of these exotic and faraway places. I guess his job has not been without risk. His company was subcontracted to fly troops into Kosova and Iraq and several times they have had 'scares' in the air; once when the plane's wind-

Sophie Grace and Phoebe Eve.

screen imploded, which caused the aircraft to drop 10,000 feet in a short space of time, and once when an engine failed. Then there was the time when an enthusiastic pilot hit the runway rather heavily and the passenger door fell off! Those things pale into insignificance when you see the crew arrive together at whatever hotel they are staying in; there are usually two lads and seven or eight gorgeous girls. I once dropped Victor off at Manchester Airport after he had been home for a couple of days. As he was booking in the remainder of the crew arrived and to hear all the crew shouting, 'Hi Vic', 'Hello darling, I am in room so and so', I could see why he had such a broad grin on his face.

I do worry about the future though and for the next generation. What do they face? But on thinking more about it I suppose our parents felt the same about us. That there will continue to be change there is no doubt, but what happens when oil runs out I shudder to think. Not only will there not be any fuel to bring in the cheap imported food, there will not be any cheap imported food, or any here either. Will that be the Armageddon we have been warned about? Will the human race destroy itself?

If anything the way ahead is even cloudier than it was before. For the first time in seventy years, there is nothing in traditional agriculture that is returning a profit. I am now writing in 2006 and a rather depressing picture is painted by the industry; in 2005 I experienced the worst harvest I have ever had in financial terms.

Dairying used to be a hardworking but profitable enterprise. It is still hardworking but with milk prices at least six or seven pence per litre cheaper to the farmer, but even dearer on the doorstep it makes a nonsense of the investment in cows. The BSE situation has not helped with cull cows worth a fraction of their previous value and calves being shot at birth as they are worth nothing. We still do not know for sure about any connection to human beings. I feel desperately sorry for those families with relatives suffering the human form but the numbers involved pale into insignificance when compared to the thousands who smoke causing themselves a lot of discomfort and ill-health as well as costing the NHS an absolute fortune. This self-inflicted misery should be banned in public everywhere. I hate having second hand smoke up my nostrils.

The whole BSE episode was an utter shambles and not really handled a lot better than the farce we endured during Foot and Mouth, hopefully never to be repeated. What an utter disgrace. Who would have thought of calves at £1 in the market - which they were at one time - meaning by the time the auctioneer took his cut, you actually owed him. A cartridge is a cheaper option but then we cannot bury them, we either have to pay the knackerman a fortune or incinerate at high cost.

Similarly with sheep, cull ewes were worthless and as one of my cousins said recently, if you see a wagon pull up near one of your fields now, you don't worry about someone stealing your sheep. You worry in case they are dumping some!

Eggs are about four pence each to the farmer, goodness knows what they cost to produce; they are twice that price at least on the shelf. Again you have to pay to get rid of cull hens, no wonder so many incinerators have been bought. Anything which dies used to have a value from the knackerman, now you pay him to have it removed for rendering. Wool is worthless and the ewe costs more to clip than the value of the fleece. Cattle have been losing a fortune since the BSE regulations came in. Cereals are being given away at around £20 per tonne, less than the cost of growing them. That is unsustainable. Sugar beet is less money than it was and anyone with C Quota will take a low price per tonne for it to go for fodder, rather than pay the financial fine imposed. Come 2007 and even the sugar quota will be cut in favour of helping Third World countries. Potatoes are either muck or money, so can't really be relied on and not all ground is suitable, and in a summer like 2004 many went to mush in the ground. Yes, there are certain farms and farmers where some sort of diversification and niche markets are possibilities, but not all farms lend themselves to that practice.

How nonsensical can we get? Milk quotas are a complete absurdity. We restrict our farmers to a tight quota, yet we import milk from France. Our own cheese factories are closing because of the shortage of milk, yet we happily import foreign cheese. How come they have surplus? Are they better at working the system than we are?

That there was an abundance of cheap meat on the Continent, there is no doubt, and particularly in the case of pig meat there was more than an abundance, the biggest portion of it illegally produced, compared with the restrictions imposed on us here. Since then there has been a reduction and one of the reasons why pig meat prices in Britain were stable if not exciting is the simple fact that meat was not so readily available at a cheap price during 2005 so that shows just how vulnerable we are. Having said that if we were to produce pig meat under the equivalent conditions found in the majority of Continental units we would end up in prison. Pig men were led down the welfare path by the supermarkets wanting everything produced under the strictest conditions, supposedly on requests from their customers. That was a laugh to start with. The majority of housewives just look at the price tag and only a handful pay lip service to welfare and they are probably vegetarians!

The retailers happily crucify us for price because of the abundance of cheap meat abroad, knowing full well that they are importing meat produced under conditions from which they would not take it from our own farms, yet they willingly admit that they have given our competitors extra time to comply. We know that Sterling is over valued by some 20% or perhaps even more which makes the purchase of imported meat a profitable option, something to do with shareholders.

I really don't know how senior executives of these companies can sleep at night, using the double standards they do and at the same time putting our own farmers out of business. I am not trained as an agony aunt, but that is precisely what I became during the pig recession with the number of farmers who made contact hoping for a glimmer of hope somewhere along the line. Many have lost their pensions, savings, life insurances and some have even lost their homes. Families have been devastated and divorces, along with suicides are at an all time high.

Who would have thought that the peace-loving, placid pig farmers of this country would one day have taken the then Minister of Agriculture, Nick Brown, to court, for his flat refusal to help the pig industry, after helping beef and sheep men? This Government must surely rank as the worst ever on record. Woe betide any country where agriculture is not encouraged - note I did not say supported as in financial support - but moral support goes a long way when there is a willingness for that country to be able to compete on a fair basis without all the red tape which keeps on appearing, and ever more and more ludicrous suggestions which throttle the very life of the rural economy. Our Government or MisGovernment, more like, has absolutely ruined the entire industry, which means the demise of the countryside, plus the failure of supply businesses to agriculture.

Farmers in France don't seem to tolerate the sort of things we do. Could it be that farming in France has a greater proportion of the voters than we have here? Our own 2% or so probably don't mean much in voting terms, but I reckon that by the time the allied industries are taken into account, we could be looking at a proportion nearer 15%. That should have some effect but it doesn't seem to. Perhaps the Government would rather pay unemployment benefit than give support to keep our nation fed, and well fed they are. There are innumerable people who rely on farming for a living. Building manufacturers, machinery dealers, engineers, joiners, garages, hauliers, millers and feed compounders, plus chemical suppliers, contractors, fertiliser manufacturers, animal health distributors and general agricultural merchants, who supply bits and pieces as well as clothing. The list is endless.

Because of the mass exodus of pig units less cereals will be required, less tonnage moved around, less feed, less veterinary work, the repercussions are enormous. Livestock markets are closing at an alarming rate and farmers are becoming more and more isolated. I have said before and will say again, 'Prosperous agriculture, prosperous country'. Farmers are the most profligate people on earth when the money is there, but by golly, nip them too hard and the wallet is put away.

We hear from Mr 'Two Jags' Prescott, who is in fact one of our local MPs and the deputy Prime Minister, that we should throw our car keys away and utilise public transport. It sounds fine in theory, but there is very little public transport in the countryside and none of it ever goes where I want to go or I suspect other farmers either. So they put up the price of fuel, which becomes an added burden. That alone puts up the cost of everything we handle, both in and out of the farm. It is a vicious circle and now the energy companies want to increase by a staggering 10-12% the cost of gas and electricity. That will have a huge impact on farming. I suppose this will be yet another cost we will not be recompensed for so it will be like another nail in the coffin lid.

The latest thing is to pay a toll on motorways and trunk roads. All that will do is increase traffic on the minor roads, and even more fuel will be used because of corners and gear changes, inevitably resulting in more road repairs. So it goes on.

We are encouraged to diversify. Not all farms lend themselves to diversification and there is a limit to the number of us who can do bed and breakfast. If you cannot diversify your farm, perhaps you can diversify yourself like I did but please don't set up another pig magazine in competition with *Pig World*!

What does the future hold? I ask myself that question repeatedly. I desperately want to be optimistic and if I had the answers I would be in great demand as a soothsayer. Frankly I know not where we are heading or what we should do.

Our colleges, so successful in the past, are struggling for agricultural students. Who are going to be the next generations of custodians of the countryside? Will it be the number of 'do-gooders' or 'Greenies', call them what you will, many whom have never set foot on a working farm? They live in a false Utopia called 'cloud-cuckoo land'.

Perhaps rather than answer that, we ought to decide whether the countryside belongs to the farmer and other people are allowed to visit, or whether it belongs to other people and we are allowed to farm it. If things carry on the way they are, I can see we will not being allowed to farm, but only to be custodians of a national park. Not many farmers are trained park keepers but having said that there are a lot of courses at the colleges these days for such an outcome. A sobering thought.

A trip to Denmark in January 2000 and again in 2001, to study the pig industry yet again, brought home to me just how important agriculture is to that country of 5 million people, who produce 400 times more pig meat than they eat. Their Government bend over backwards to help the social structure of family farming to continue. It is vitally important to them. It makes our lot of political pygmies look what they are, totally oblivious to the obvious, that farming should be kept on a profitable level.

I know our pig farmers get a bit uptight about the Danes, but they are actually sending us less now than they have done for the last decade. It is not so much the Danes who are creating the problem it is other nations like the Dutch, French, Irish, Spanish and Poles on the pig meat side. Are we soon to be invaded by the Americans and the Canadians? Maybe not directly, but if meat is so cheap to produce over there, perhaps they will conquer the Far Eastern outlets, leaving more European stuff to be dumped on our shores. I believe Brazil poses a danger. There, along with Vietnam, is the cheapest country in which to produce pig and poultry meat. The fact that the disease status leaves a lot to be desired seems to be irrelevant.

The whole concept of agriculture and with it, a way of life has changed so dramatically as to be virtually unrecognisable. That in itself has been a problem. But I believe the bigger problem is yet to come, and that is the changes or adaptability we are going to see and will have to survive in the current decade, let alone century, from global trading rather than rural trading.

I note we are currently laying up our naval ships as they are costing too much in fuel to operate. I wonder if the time will ever come when the same thing will happen to merchant shipping if the price of oil keeps rising? Now that would make a mess of imports! Now't like a bit of hunger to create a bit of unrest.

The longer I farm the more confused I become. New red tape, rules and regulations, the three R's (not reading, writing and 'rithmetic) are frightening the older generation who simply cannot cope. The move to the Single Farm Payment scheme was for many the last straw. It was made so complicated and the cross compliance too. Each year we seem to have yet a different approach to what is allowed. The decision to take the three years, 2000, 2001 and 2002 as the base years to average out farm payments was ill-conceived and caused endless problems for many farmers. They were almost afraid to fill in the forms in case they committed a crime and could be fined retrospectively. Since when could you fine a criminal for a law, which was not even thought of when the supposed crime was committed? Again the scheme was being administered by people on fat salaries and pensions that would not be affected by anything they did and certainly not by anything they did to farming. I am absolutely sure that they nit-pick round the edges of the rules or so-called rules because they are absolutely sure that farmers are on the fiddle.

As nice as it might be to see strips of wild flowers round the edges of fields and acres of wild bird cover, it doesn't particularly gladden a farmer's heart to see land producing 'nowt' when all his life he has been expected to produce food. I think the industry has been the victim of its own success. I had a chap tell not me on the very day that I was writing this that he felt the public, who have been misled over subsidies for food, would probably be happy to see farmers paid a basic wage in return for keeping the countryside tidy. Part of the problem is going to be China. One sixth of the world's population, laying 50% of the world's concrete, has caused the price of steel to double as they build factories to utilise cheap labour. They will achieve two things. Firstly, the West will be conquered economically, and second, the younger generation who are flocking in droves from the countryside to work in manufacturing, are going to find that when the older generation have retired or died, there will be no one to run the thousands of small peasant farms which supplies whole communities with the basics of life. They will have to be fed from somewhere and already China has gobbled up any surplus soya meal from Brazil to feed their expanding pig and poultry farms and for human consumption too. That means Brazil chops down more rain forests, in turn affecting the ozone layer and global warming. Each year we lose thousands of acres to not only soil and coast erosion, but to housing, factories, motorways and other roads. The possibilities are frightening.

We had the SARS outbreak in China, and we had a disease in Indonesia caused by the Nipar virus that is carried by the fruit bat which killed many pigs and not a few humans. Avian 'flu is rampant particularly in Thailand, and some fifty people have died from that. Should it mutate into other species of live-stock and to more humans what happens then? Maybe that is nature's way of evening out life and our critical resources.

We cannot and must not rely totally on other countries to supply us with cheap food. In a real world there is no such thing. Apart from being financial suicide it is an insult to the finest farmers in the world who are in an industry, which is a bit like life, somewhat of a lottery or perhaps more like buying a pig in a poke!

Clio Publishing is a young company with a growing reputation for providing bespoke publishing solutions for authors and researchers in the arts and humanities. The incredible flexibility, speed, and cost-efficiency of print-on-demand technology combined with the marketing opportunities of the internet and direct mail, now offer authors a powerful new way of exploiting their intellectual property.

If you are an author in the arts and humanities that would like to take charge of your publishing destiny, please contact in the first instance Dr Susan England at info@cliopublishing.co.uk or telephone +44 (0) 23 8058 4460. You can also view the Clio Publishing website at www.cliopublishing.co.uk